Worldliness infects us deepe[...]
It seeks to inhabit our perce[...]
starts in the heart. Anthony S[...]
pulse of a worldly age, and his[...]
idolatry of our hearts in such reigning ideas as individualism, consumerism, relativism, obsession with the new, and
contempt for the past. Like a good doctor, Selvaggio does
not rail at us about our illness; he aims to heal and so offers
solutions in Christ. Whether you are a teenager, a mother, a
businessman, or a pastor, this book will bring health to your
soul and equip you to live soberly, righteously, and godly in
this present world.
> —**Joel R. Beeke,** president, Puritan Reformed Theological
> Seminary, Grand Rapids

Anthony Selvaggio's topics are timely and will certainly
be of help to many. His writing style is engaging and easy
to read. While popularly written, he demonstrates a depth
of research in the footnotes. Selvaggio underlines the
importance of a consistent biblical worldview and warns
his readers against false worldviews that are attractive.
Highly recommended.
> —**Richard C. Gamble,** professor of systematic theology,
> Reformed Presbyterian Theological Seminary, Pittsburgh

By making good things ultimate things—love becomes
lust, rest becomes sloth, and so on—we fall into what used
to be called the seven deadly sins. We have a harder time
spotting the seven modern idolatries that Anthony Selvaggio outlines for us, but the process is similar: individuality
becomes individualism, equal opportunity becomes egalitarianism, and so on. *7 Toxic Ideas Polluting Your Mind* helps
us to spot those current tendencies and, with God's grace,
contain them.
> —**Marvin Olasky**, editor-in-chief, *WORLD* magazine

Anthony Selvaggio's book should not be overlooked by thoughtful Christians. He challenges the incorrect notion that "worldliness" constitutes merely overt behavior, and he rightly reminds us that our thoughts and ideas end up shaping our behaviors far more than we think. He rightly uncovers seven common ideas/values in American culture that are contrary to the principles disclosed in Holy Scripture.

—**T. David Gordon**, professor of religion and Greek, Grove City College, Grove City, Pennsylvania

7 TOXIC IDEAS POLLUTING YOUR MIND

7 TOXIC IDEAS POLLUTING YOUR MIND

Anthony Selvaggio

P&R
PUBLISHING
P.O. BOX 817 • PHILLIPSBURG • NEW JERSEY 08865-0817

Library of Congress Cataloging-in-Publication Data

Selvaggio, Anthony T.
  7 toxic ideas polluting your mind / Anthony Selvaggio.
      p. cm.
  Includes bibliographical references.
  ISBN 978-1-59638-196-4 (pbk.)
  1. Ideology--Religious aspects--Christianity. 2. Christian life--Reformed Presbyterian authors. I. Title. II. Title: Seven toxic ideas polluting your mind.
  BR115.I35S45 2011
  261--dc23
                                    2011037275

To my friend
Russell Pulliam

for his editorial and journalistic insights,
which significantly improved this book

Contents

Foreword

CHRISTIANS HAVE ALWAYS been concerned about the problem of worldliness. From Athanasius' ancient cry, "*Contra Mundum*" ("Against the World"), to the modern evangelical cliché, "Be *in* the world, but not *of* the world," Christians have long struggled to resist conformity to the world around them. In modern evangelicalism, however, the tendency has been to see this struggle as dealing primarily with external behavior. That is, as long as Christians avoid a specified list of external behavior practices, then they are not conforming to the world. But this approach to avoiding worldliness has had a devastating impact on the church. While external behavior practices do matter, the real battle to avoid worldliness occurs internally, in our hearts and minds. While we have been consumed with external matters, worldliness has gained a foothold in our thought processes. Satan has been very successful in getting us to *think* like the world. This book is an effort to counter Satan's attack on our minds. It's a counterinsurgency aimed at thwarting the evil intentions of our adversary.

1

Ideas to Idolatry

Ideas Have Consequences

Absorption in ease is one of the most reliable signs of present or impending decay.
—Richard M. Weaver

HE WAS BORN on April 20, 1889 in what was then known as Austria-Hungary. As a young man, he fought in World War I and was decorated for his valor in service to his country. After the war, he entered politics and launched a failed coup against the leadership in Germany. For this transgression he was imprisoned. After his release, he wrote a book bearing the title *Mein Kampf*. That man, of course, was Adolf Hitler, and his little book, and the dreadful ideas it contained, altered the course of the entire twentieth century and led to the death of millions.

Ideas are powerful things. On the one hand, ideas can lead to wonderful developments such as democracy, cures for illnesses, and putting a man on the moon. But ideas can also lead to devastating atrocities such as Communism, Nazism, genocide, and slavery. While ideas can be both good and bad, they are rarely, if ever, neutral or indifferent. As the twentieth-century philosopher Richard M. Weaver reminded us in his 1948 book, ideas have consequences.

The consequences of ideas become even more powerful when these ideas morph into a comprehensive ideology, or *worldview*. A worldview attempts to provide a comprehensive understanding of reality. When an idea becomes a worldview, it can alter the entire course of a civilization. Consider, for example, the altering power of such worldviews as Nazism and Communism.

For Christians, this matter of ideas and worldviews takes on an even greater significance because embracing the wrong ideas or worldview can lead us to worship and serve false gods. In other words, ideas can lead to idolatry. Ideas become idolatrous when they are contrary to God's Word. When worldly ideas replace God's Word as our intellectual and moral guidance systems, we are heading down the path to idolatry. Ideas do have consequences—even eternal consequences.

The purpose of this book is to expose seven particular ideas that are undermining our culture, the church, and the Christian mind. These seven ideas are akin to the golden calf that Israel crafted in the wilderness. They are opportunities for idolatry. The question for us is whether we will choose to embrace these ideas indiscriminately or take every one of them captive for Christ.

Of course, every Christian will enthusiastically endorse the latter of these two courses of action. We all want to reject ideas that are contrary to a God-centered worldview, but unfortunately this task is not as easy as it might seem. Bad ideas often come in attractive and subtle packaging. They are not like cigarette packs: they do not have black-box warning labels describing their hidden dangers. In addition, behind these ideas stands a great foe who longs to seduce us into accepting ideas that are contrary to God's Word. Satan is ultimately behind all ideas that attempt to undermine our minds. He is, after all, the Father of Lies, and he will try to deceive us. He also has the benefit of having two great advantages over us that make our efforts to resist his lies even more challenging.

The Advantages of the Adversary

Advantage #1: He's Crafty

The first advantage that Satan has over us is his cleverness. Genesis 3:1 notes that the serpent was "*more crafty* than any of the wild animals that the Lord God had made." In other words, Satan is shrewd, cunning, and manipulative. In fact, he is so crafty and persuasive in presenting his worldview that he was able to deceive Adam and Eve *before* the fall when their minds were not yet disabled by sin. The point is that Satan is "more crafty" than we are, and we must not underestimate his ability to deceive us. Remember, unlike Adam and Eve, our minds *are* disabled by sin. If Satan was crafty enough to deceive Adam and Eve before the fall, just think how easy it is for him to deceive those who are impacted by the fall. Our minds are darkened by sin. We see through a glass darkly. Our minds are not enlightened like noonday; rather, they are in the fog of twilight. Satan is crafty and we are disabled. Never forget that he is a master of disguise. He is gifted in making evil take on the appearance of good. He masquerades as "an angel of light" (2 Cor. 11:14). This is why we so easily conform ourselves to the principles of this world, to the worldview of Satan.

Advantage #2: He's Got a Foothold

Satan's second advantage over us is his tremendous foothold on the mind-set of this world. The world accepts Satan's bad ideas as truth, and this means that you must engage in an offensive mental war that involves tearing down his strongholds. Paul describes this advantage of Satan in Ephesians 2:2, where he refers to Satan as the "ruler of the kingdom of the air." Now, Paul is not saying here that Satan and his minions are floating around in the air; rather, he is telling us that Satan's worldview pervades our very atmosphere. His worldview is in the air we breathe. We cannot escape it because we live in it and the people around us accept it. His worldview is all-pervasive. It is preached from pulpits, it echoes in the chambers of government, it resounds from the lecterns of the university, and it is broadcast through every conceivable form of media. In other words, we are constantly being inundated by Satan's worldview—we are utterly surrounded.

This advantage of the adversary not only means that we must take ground from him, but also means that we must be on guard against absorbing his worldview by mere mental osmosis. Because we are surrounded and inundated by his worldview, it is very easy to simply accept it without any active mental choice. Buying in to his ideas requires only that we take the lazy path of least resistance. As Richard Weaver noted, all we need to begin on the pathway to idolatry is "absorption in ease."

The challenge for the Christian is to avoid being taken captive by the worldview of Satan. We must avoid being fooled by a foe that is much wiser, and more cunning, than we are. We must also filter the very air we breathe so as not to assimilate into our thinking the subtle wickedness of the kingdom of the air and the spirit of this age. Our challenge is to avoid being conformed to this world. The apostle Paul summarizes this challenge in Romans 12:2: "Do not conform any longer to the pattern of this world, but be transformed by the renewing of your mind." This is the essence of our challenge.

Meeting the Challenge: A Strategy for Success

To meet this challenge, the Christian must go on the offensive. We simply can't be passive in this struggle. Passivity will lead to defeat. As Christians, we are called to pick up intellectual arms and join the battle for the mind. But before we enter into battle, we need a plan for victory. Thankfully, the Bible gives us such a plan, and it is a simple one. In order to secure victory, we must first identify the enemy and then demolish him by taking his ideas captive to Christ.

Identifying the Enemy: Understanding the Times

If we are to properly identify the enemy, we must become like the men of Issachar. Who were these men? The men of Issachar joined in support of King David as he asserted his kingship over Israel in opposition to Saul. The men of Issachar recognized that David was Israel's true ruler. They were wise men. Scripture describes them as men "who understood the times and knew what Israel should do" (1 Chron. 12:32). The men of Issachar were able to see through the fog of current events and discern God's will. They were able to decipher the code of the world in which they lived, and they understood how to respond to it. We must become like the men of Issachar. We must become like Moses in Egypt and Daniel in Babylon. We must realize that we live as sheep among wolves and thus must be as shrewd as serpents (Matt. 10:16). We must read our culture and understand our times to identify the enemy. This book will assist you in doing this with each of the seven ideas it presents.

Demolishing the Enemy: Taking Every Thought Captive

Once the enemy has been identified, we must then demolish him. The apostle Paul issues the following rule of engagement in 2 Corinthians 10:5: "We demolish arguments and every pretension that sets itself up against the knowledge of God, and we take captive every thought to make it obedient to Christ." Here Paul tells us that after we identify the enemy, after we discern the arguments and ideas that are contrary to the knowledge of God, we must then "demolish" them. Paul's command, however, is not tantamount to a "take no prisoners" policy. Rather, he calls us to demolish our enemy by taking his ideas captive and making them submissive to Christ: "we take captive every thought to make it obedient to Christ." We demolish the enemy by dismantling his arguments and exposing the wickedness of his pretensions. Our calling is to intellectually disarm, neutralize, and transform the enemy.

To do this, however, we must not rely on our own wit because, as we have seen, the serpent is "more crafty" than we are. Therefore, instead of relying on our wit, we demolish our enemy by employing the only offensive weapon in Paul's inventory of the armor of God in Ephesians 6—we use "the sword of the Spirit, which is the word of God" (Eph. 6:17). We can demolish the enemy only when we engage him as Jesus engaged him. During his temptation in the wilderness, Jesus confronted the Scripture-twisting and lies of Satan, and he demolished his arguments not with his own clever argumentation, but with the very Word of God. Each time Satan confronted Jesus with an argument and pretension that was contrary to the knowledge of God, Jesus demolished it by responding with these three words: "it is written" (Matt. 4:4, 6, 7, 10). The only way we will be successful in destroying the enemy, demolishing his arguments, and taking them captive to Christ is by wielding the weapon of the Word of God. This book will assist you in doing this with each of these seven ideas.

Engaging the Enemy

As we've seen in this chapter, the Christian is engaged in a constant and epic intellectual struggle against a formidable adversary. The call to the Christian in the midst of this great conflict is a call to arms. It is a call to join the battle, to engage in the war of the worldviews. God calls us to identify the enemy by understanding the times and to demolish the enemy by using the Word of God. He calls us to resist allowing ideas to become idolatry.

Now that we have our marching orders and understand our mission, it's time for us to engage the enemy.

2

Technopoly

The iPod Nation

*Then they said, "Come, let us build ourselves a
city, with a tower that reaches to the heavens, so
that we may make a name for ourselves and not
be scattered over the face of the whole earth."*
(Gen. 11:4)

A FEW YEARS AGO I asked my wife for a portable GPS for
Christmas. The main purpose of this particular GPS device is
to prevent one from getting lost when hiking, camping, hunt-
ing, or fishing. It allows you to mark your beginning point and
then electronically retrace your steps back to that point. It's
the high-tech equivalent of Hansel and Gretel's bread-crumb
system. In other words, it's really neat! The humorous thing,
however, was that I had absolutely no need for this device! I
don't hike, camp, hunt, or fish. At the time I received the gift, I
was not even at risk of getting lost on my way to work because
I worked five hundred feet from my home! I had no practical
need for this device. So why did I want it? I wanted it because

it's really neat! Like many other people in our culture, I suffer from *technophilia*—the love of technology.

Now, there's nothing wrong with technology per se. In fact, to the contrary—there are many things *right* about technology. Technology has brought tremendous blessings to our world, such as vaccines, agricultural advances, and indoor plumbing. Even Neil Postman, a critic of the effects of technology, noted that it would be "stupid to be anti-technology. That would be something like being anti-food. We need technology to live, as we need food to live."[1] But Postman also qualified that statement by cautioning, "But, of course, if we eat too much food, or eat food that has no nutritional value, or eat food that is infected with disease, we turn a means of survival into its opposite. The same may be said of our technology."[2] Therefore, what I am confronting in this chapter is not technology itself, but the harmful effects that result from its misuse and overuse. I am confronting what Postman referred to as *technopoly*, which he defined as a "state of culture" and a "state of mind" that "consists in the deification of technology, finds its satisfaction in technology, and takes its orders from technology."[3] Technopoly occurs when technology dominates and controls our lives.

What I want you to see in this chapter is that technology can be used by Satan to undermine your allegiance to God. When use of technology morphs into technopoly, it becomes an idol, an enemy. In this chapter, we will explore the effects of technopoly and how to counter them.

The Biblical Worldview: Discernment Required

At first, we might think the Bible doesn't address the topic of technology. After all, we generally consider technology an

1. Neil Postman, *Building a Bridge to the Eighteenth Century* (New York: Alfred Knopf, 2001), 44.
2. Ibid.
3. Neil Postman, *Technopoly: The Surrender of Culture to Technology* (New York: Vintage Books, 1993), 71.

aspect of our modern world. When we think of technology, we think of computers, cell phones, and so forth. Of course, none of these devices existed in biblical times. That does not mean, however, that the Bible is void of guidance on how to properly engage and use technology to God's glory. To the contrary, the Bible gives us two principles that will help us to avoid the ill effects of technopoly.

Principle #1: It's about Motivations

In the book of Genesis, God commands humanity to subdue the earth for his glory. The development and use of technology are obviously necessary to fulfill this great mandate. Therefore, the Bible does not call the Christian to abandon or avoid technology. Instead, it calls us to embrace it for the glory of God. What God is concerned about is not the development and use of technology, but the motivations behind its development and use. Therefore, when it comes to our use of technology, we must first do a motivation check and ask ourselves *why* we wish to use it. Two examples will illustrate this point.

First, consider Noah. Noah was a righteous man, and God called him to engage in a massive technological enterprise—he told Noah to build an ark. This was the greatest technological endeavor the world had seen at that point. But consider Noah's motivations in building the ark. He was predominantly motivated by a desire to obey and serve God. He was also motivated by a desire to save himself, his family, and, in a sense, creation itself. Through his use of technology, he was showing love to both God and his neighbor.

Now contrast Noah's motivations for using technology with those of the Babelites. In Genesis 11:4, we learn that the Babelites decided to build a massive tower that would reach to the heavens. As was Noah's ark, the tower was a Herculean technological endeavor. But unlike the motivation of Noah, the Babelites' motivation for engaging in this technological effort was not to love God and their neighbor, but rather to make a name for themselves (Gen. 11:4). In other words, they wanted to climb into the heavens to dethrone God and become gods themselves. This is why God came down and confused their efforts. Bruce Waltke comments as follows on the Babelites' misuse of technology:

> Technology, which enables human beings to subdue the earth and in part sets them above the animals, is God's good gift to people. However, people pervert it. Since the word *name* connotes fame and progeny, the city builders were futilely attempting to find significance and immortality in their technology and their achievements. But technology cannot give divine blessing. Only God can give an everlasting name (see Gen. 12:2), and he gives it to those who magnify his name and not their own achievements.[4]

The Babelites serve as a stark reminder of how the use of technology can lead us into technopoly.

When it comes to our use of technology, the Bible instructs us to do a heart check. It calls us to examine our motivations and ask ourselves why we are using technology. We need to ask ourselves whether the chief end of our use of technology is to glorify God and enjoy him forever. It's all about our motivations.

Principle #2: It's about Moderation

Proverbs 25:27 contains this great morsel of wisdom: "It is not good to eat too much honey." The meaning of this counsel is immediately apparent to any person who has overindulged in food or drink of any kind. In fact, my own daughter has this particular struggle of overindulgence in honey. She desires to put honey on everything and in great portions! I often have to

---

4. Bruce Waltke, *Genesis* (Grand Rapids: Zondervan, 2001), 183. Derek Kidner comments similarly, "The elements of the story are timelessly characteristic of the spirit of the world. The project is typically grandiose; men describe it excitedly to one another as if it were the ultimate achievement—very much as modern man glories in his space projects." Derek Kidner, *Genesis* (Downers Grove, IL: InterVarsity Press, 1967), 109.

remind her of the simple point of this proverb: you can have too much of a good thing. The same is true for our use of technology.

Technology is much like honey in our culture. Honey is an enjoyable thing that doesn't contain a great deal of nourishment. Because it is tasty and sweet, we often want more and more of it, but it really doesn't contribute much to our physical well-being. Technology in our culture often functions in a similar way. Most of the technology we engage with is related to some form of entertainment. Technology allows us to watch videos, engage in social networking, play games, and shop. These are not bad things; rather, like honey, they are quite enjoyable. But these technological forms of entertainment are also like honey in the sense that they don't really offer us much spiritual nutrition. Remember the admonition of Paul to the Philippians: "Finally, brothers, whatever is true, whatever is noble, whatever is right, whatever is pure, whatever is lovely, whatever is admirable—if anything is excellent or praiseworthy—think about such things" (Phil. 4:8). God calls us to become consumed with things that will nourish our souls. The danger for us is that because technology can offer us such a sweet and enjoyable experience, we can often engage in it to excess. The Bible reminds us that all things should be used in moderation, and this particularly applies to our use of technology.

When it comes to using technology, a biblical worldview requires that we do a heart check (whereby we evaluate our motivations for using it) and a gut check (whereby we evaluate our appetites to see whether we are overusing it). In other words, a biblical worldview requires us to ask ourselves *why* we are using technology and *how much* we are using it.

The Worldview of the Adversary: Embrace Technopoly

In contrast to this biblical worldview of technology, our adversary desires to see us violate both of these biblical principles. He desires us to behave like the Babelites and to eat all the honey we want. He desires to see us succumb to technopoly. He does this by encouraging us to use technology to become disengaged, distracted, and disembodied.

Disengagement

The twentieth-century poet and cultural critic T. S. Eliot noted that one of the problems facing the modern world is fragmentation. Eliot realized that technology had the potential to destroy community. In 1934, in a poem entitled "The Rock," Eliot wrote the following:

> What life have you, if you have not life together?
> There is not life that is not in community,
> And no community not lived in praise of GOD.
> And now you live dispersed on ribbon roads,
> And no man knows or cares who is his neighbor
> Unless his neighbor makes too much disturbance,
> But all dash to and fro in motor cars,
> Familiar with the roads and settled nowhere.[5]

Eliot feared that the technological development of the automobile would disengage people from their neighbors. Of course, history proved Eliot correct. The disconnected and anonymous suburbs of our modern world were made possible by the automobile.

The threat of the disengaging power of technology has only heightened in the twenty-first century. While technological developments such as cell phones and the Internet have been lauded as a means of fostering greater connectivity in our world, ironically they have often delivered exactly the opposite. Technology frequently disengages us from our real three-dimensional world and connects us to an unreal two-

5. T.S. Eliot, *Complete Poems and Plays: 1909–1950* (Harcourt Brace & Company: Orlando, FL, 1971), 101–2.

dimensional virtual world. By disengaging us from the context of our real world, technology subtly robs us of meaningful interaction with our neighbor.

Consider, for example, the practice of online shopping. At one level, online shopping is a tremendous convenience. There is no need to drive to the store, fight over a parking space, and deal with the crowds in the shopping mall. Sounds great, doesn't it? Where's the downside in this? But think about what is lost in online shopping. What is lost is community. When you shop online, you have no opportunity to relate to other human beings. You can't help that young mother struggling to put her child into a stroller. You can't assist that elderly woman with her packages. You can't share your faith with the person sitting next to you in the food court. The virtual world disengages us from the real world, from real people.

I remember the first time I encountered someone who was wearing a cell-phone earpiece. I was waiting in line at Starbucks, and this man in front of me seemed to be talking to himself. At first, I thought he was mentally unstable, and so I cautiously backed away from him. But then I saw the device protruding from his ear. The man proceeded to carry on a cell-phone conversation the entire time he was in Starbucks. My guess is that he never even noticed the other humans around him. He was entirely disengaged from the context of his real-world surroundings. He was there, but he wasn't there. Social scientists have coined the term *absent presence* to describe this phenomenon. If you have ever tried to have a conversation with a teenager who is compulsively texting his or her friends, you will fully understand the meaning of this term. Technology enables absent presence, and it is a tool that allows us to easily and dangerously disengage from the real world.

This type of technologically induced disengagement has real spiritual implications for the church. Jesus commands us to love our neighbors as ourselves (Luke 10:27) and to share the gospel with every creature (Matt. 28:18–20). We can't love our neighbor and we can't share the gospel if we refuse to engage our world. In our culture, we are plugging in and tuning out. Our slavish devotion to technology is disengaging us from the real world of hurting people. This is exactly what Satan wants us to do. He wants us to neglect our neighbor. Think about it—if the Good Samaritan had been wearing an iPod and text-messaging his friend on a cell phone, do you think he would have noticed the wounded man in the ditch? Technology can be used as a means of disengaging us from our world. Are you suffering from this symptom of technopoly? Are you using technology to disengage from the real world around you?

Distraction

In Ray Bradbury's classic novel *Fahrenheit 451*, he depicts a world in which people are obsessed with watching wall-sized television screens. This obsession is encouraged by the government, and it is used as a means of distracting people from their lives, particularly from the fact that they are living under tyranny.[6] In Bradbury's novel, the entertaining distraction of technology is used to enslave the hearts and minds of people. Distraction is a symptom of technopoly.

The primary way in which technology distracts us from what's really important is by entertaining us. As Neil Postman has pointed out, technology has enhanced our opportunities to amuse ourselves to death. Technology has exponentially increased our ability to entertain ourselves. Thanks to technology, we can play video games, watch DVDs, and listen to downloaded digital music—simultaneously!

Of course, entertainment is not inherently evil. Entertainment is a legitimate form of recreation. It becomes harmful, however, when it dominates our lives and distracts us

---

6. It is interesting to note how our culture is slowly fulfilling Bradbury's prophecy issued more than a half-century ago. Some of the hottest products in the entertainment industry are large-screen flat-panel televisions that are mounted on the walls of our homes.

from focusing on the truly important things, such as our relationship with God. When entertainment dominates our lives, it creates what the French sociologist and theologian Jacques Ellul referred to as "empty time," which causes people to "lose their sense of reality and to abandon their search for truth."[7]

Satan loves to distract us. He is quite pleased to satisfy our minds and consume our lives by offering us endless sources of entertainment. He wants to fill our lives with empty time. He understands that distractions and diversions work in his favor. He knows what the French theologian Blaise Pascal knew: "All the major forms of diversion are dangerous to the Christian life."[8] The last thing Satan wants you to do is to fulfill the admonition of Paul to "set your minds on things above" (Col. 3:2). One of the ways he keeps you from doing this is through the distracting power of technology. Are you suffering from this symptom of technopoly? Are you using technology to distract you from what's really important?

Disembodiment

God created us as unified beings possessing both body and soul. This vital union is what defines us as human. Technology, however, has made it possible for us to divide this vital union of body and soul. Through technology, a person is able to be consciously present in a virtual world without his or her body going along for the ride. Technology allows disembodied consciousness. The philosopher Albert Borgman notes that technology allows a person to receive information solely through eyes and ears while the rest of the body becomes both "immobile and irrelevant." Borgman notes that the end result

---

7. Jacques Ellul, *The Technological Society*, trans. John Wilkinson (New York: Random House, 1964), 337, quoted in Marva Dawn, *Unfettered Hope* (Louisville, KY: Westminster John Knox Press, 2003), 18.

8. Blaise Pascal, *Pensées*, trans. A. J. Krailsheimer (New York: Penguin, 1966), pensée no. 764, quoted in Dawn, *Unfettered Hope*, 19.

of this process is a "disembodied person."[9] Never before in human history have humans had the ability to separate their consciousness from their bodies.

This disembodiment is spiritually dangerous because it makes us both less human and less humane. The separation of our consciousness from our bodies allows us to also separate our actions from our bodies. When humans are able to separate their bodies from their actions, they are more likely to engage in sinful and destructive behavior because they can distance themselves from the consequences of their actions. In other words, technological disembodiment leads us to engage in activities that we would never engage in if our whole being were present. Here are a couple examples of how the danger of disembodiment manifests itself in the virtual world of our day.

First, consider the rampant immodesty displayed on the Internet. The Internet has brought emotional and physical exhibitionism to an entirely new level. It's not just the publicity-seeking celebrities who are baring their most intimate details on the Internet; teenage boys and girls are getting into the act as well. One recent study found that more than half of U.S. teenagers use social networking sites such as Facebook to share their personal information.[10] Young people in our culture now routinely place the most intimate details about themselves in cyberspace for the entire world to see. They share with millions of strangers, some of whom are sexual predators, things they would never share in a face-to-face conversation with another human being. Many are engaging in what is referred to as *sexting*, which involves the sharing of lurid personal digital photos with others. Why is this type of rank immodesty occurring? Because technology

9. Albert Borgman, *Crossing the Postmodern Divide* (Chicago: University of Chicago Press, 1992), 106, quoted in Dawn, *Unfettered Hope*, 4.

10. From a study conducted by the Pew Internet & American Life Project, results reported in an article entitled "Study: On MySpace, Girls Seek Friends, Boys Flirt," January 8, 2007, www.cnn.com.

allows us to become disembodied, it allows us to separate our virtual actions from our real bodies.

Second, think about the incipient incivility displayed on the Internet. Schoolchildren now trash their classmates in virtual Internet communities, a practice that is known as *cyberbullying.*[11] Young people are ruining the reputations of real people by their disembodied actions in the virtual world. They display a level of cruelty in this virtual world that they would never express in real-world encounters. Adults engage in similar sordid behavior through a phenomenon known as *webtribution,* in which one person is berated and slandered through e-mail, social networking, or blogs by someone who desires to tear that person down. This type of cyberattack on the reputations of others also occurs among Christians. Unfortunately, it is most prevalent among ministers. Theologians and pastors frequently use e-mail and blogs as the means of accusing one another of all forms of sins and theological errors. Heresy trials now occur with a few strokes of the keyboard. Why is this type of cruel behavior occurring and escalating in the culture and the church? Because the Internet allows people to separate their bodies from their actions, it allows them to put a virtual wall of separation between themselves and the image of God that they are attacking.

We must remember that Satan seeks to distort the structure and direction of God's creation. God made us a unified creature, and therefore Satan seeks to divide us. He realizes that if he can divide us, then he can conquer us. One of the ways he divides the essence of our being is through the subtle disembodying power of technology. Are you suffering from this symptom of technopoly? Are you using technology to become disembodied as you engage your consciousness in the virtual world without consequences?

11. Anne Marie Chaker, "Schools Act to Short-Circuit Spread of 'Cyberbullying,'" *Wall Street Journal,* January 24, 2007.

It is true that technology is a tool to build and create things, but it can also become a tool to destroy things. It can destroy our communities through disengagement, our relationship with God through distraction, and our sense of morality through disembodiment.

Resisting Technopoly

In this chapter, we have seen the harmful effects of technopoly demonstrated both in the Bible and in our own lives. But our use of technology need not degenerate into technopoly. Technopoly can be resisted. To faithfully resist it, however, we must engage in the very activities that it seeks to destroy. We must engage our world, pay attention to the important things, and remain embodied when online.

Engage the Real World

Technological disengagement can be resisted by simply engaging our real world. We must put limits on our use of technology. We must use this good gift in moderation. It means that we must set aside times when we are not hooked up to some machine. We must turn off our televisions, computers, cell phones, and other personal technological devices and engage other human beings in meaningful face-to-face conversations. We must regularly turn off the virtual world and tune in to our real world.

Instead of spending endless hours "blogging" with the faceless masses of the digital world, strike up a conversation with one real flesh-and-blood person. Instead of sending an abbreviated text message filled with cyberacronyms, take the time to speak to someone in carefully considered complete sentences and paragraphs. Instead of endlessly counting your so-called virtual "friends" on Facebook, focus on cultivating a deep friendship with one or two people who attend your church or live within your local community. In other words, pull the iPod earbuds out of your ears and begin to become aware of the world around you. Endeavor to love and know your neighbor. Strive to become aware of the aliens who are constantly entering the gates of your world. Instead of participating in a virtual community, engage your real community, especially the local covenant community of your church.

Pay Attention

We can resist technological distraction by becoming more attentive to the important things in life. This means that we must regularly give our undivided attention to our relationship with God. Again we must turn off and tune in. Instead of constantly being distracted by multimedia, make time to be singularly focused on God. Like the psalmist, meditate on God's unfailing love (Ps. 48:9), his mighty deeds (77:12), and his awesome Word (119:97).

Meditation is a powerful weapon in the fight against technopoly because it is entirely anti-technological. While technology has provided us with many helpful tools to study God's Word, true communion with God cannot be achieved through technological devices. You simply can't Google your way to spiritual maturity. So disconnect from Facebook and make some space, and some time, for paying attention to what really matters—your relationship with God.

Remain Embodied

Technological disembodiment can be resisted by refusing to divorce your actions from your body. You must remain embodied online, and you can accomplish this by adopting some simple principles to govern your involvement with the virtual world.

First, when you're online, embody the principle of virtual modesty. In 1 Corinthians 12:23, the apostle Paul notes that there are parts of our bodies that are "unpresentable" and should therefore be treated with "special modesty." That special modesty is exercised by covering our "unpresentable" parts. We honor these parts by privatizing them. While Paul was addressing our physical bodies, this principle of modesty also extends to other intimate aspects of our lives. Therefore, make it a rule to never put intimate details about your life, or the lives of others, on the Internet. Treat these most intimate details with special modesty. Don't allow yourself to become disembodied through virtual immodesty.

Second, when you're online, embody the principle of virtual civility. Establish rules to govern your electronic discourse. For instance, make it a rule to never say anything cruel about another person on the Internet. Prohibit yourself from engaging in cybergossip, cyberbullying, and webtribution. Let the Golden Rule guide all your actions on the Internet: "In everything, do to others what you would have them do to you" (Matt. 7:12). Don't allow yourself to become disembodied through virtual incivility.

If you desire to avoid the onset of technopoly in your life, then you must actively resist it. You must control your use of technology. Instead of becoming disengaged, engage your real world. Instead of becoming distracted, pay attention to what's truly important. Instead of becoming disembodied, become embodied by never morally divorcing your actions from your body in the virtual world. This is how you resist technopoly in your life.

The Lesson of the Luddites

In the nineteenth century, a group of garment workers violently opposed the introduction of mechanization in England's garment industry. They attempted to resist technological progress by destroying the machines that were seeking to replace their labor. The resistance displayed by this group was referred to as the *Luddite movement*. Today, the term *Luddite* is used pejoratively to refer to a person who opposes technological advances. Most people think the lesson to be learned from the Luddites is that it is foolish to oppose technological progress.

But Neil Postman has noted that the real lesson is not that opposing technology is foolish, but rather that technological advances produce both winners and losers. Postman's point is that every advance in technology gives us something, but it also takes away something from us. Technology took away the livelihood of the Luddites, and it has the potential to take away things from you as well. Jesus warns us that things can cost us our soul: "What good will it be for a man if he gains the whole world, yet forfeits his soul?" (Matt. 16:26).

It is vital for Christians, particularly Christian parents, to realize that the use of technology has spiritual implications. Therefore, a wise Christian recognizes this reality and thus becomes a shrewd and discerning user of technology. A wise Christian counts the cost of his use of technology and never allows it to become a weapon in the hands of Satan. So next time you plug in, turn on, log on, or boot up, think about whether you are using technology or whether it is using you.

3

Neophilia

"History Is Bunk"

Those who leave the tradition of truth do not escape into something which we call Freedom. They only escape into something else, which we call Fashion.
—G. K. Chesterton[1]

THE TWENTIETH-CENTURY industrialist Henry Ford is most well known for the development of the Model T automobile. But Ford is also known for a famous statement he made about history: "History is bunk." Ford didn't say it in those exact words; what he actually said was: "History is more or less bunk. It's tradition. We don't want tradition. We want to live in the present, and the only history that is worth a tinker's damn is the history that we make today."[2]

Henry Ford was a man enamored of the future, a future that he desired to shape in his own image. For Ford, tradition

---

1. G.K. Chesterton, *Collected Works of G. K. Chesterton*, vol. 3 (Ignatius Press: San Francisco, 1990), 388.
2. Interview in *Chicago Tribune*, May 25, 1916.

served only as a stumbling block to progress. Ford believed that new things are always better than old things. This mindset of Henry Ford is very much alive in our world. We live in a culture that is infatuated with all things new. Our culture suffers from neophilia.

Neophilia simply means "love of the new." Those who suffer from this insatiable love of new things are referred to as *neophiliacs* or *neophiles*. These terms are most frequently used in our culture to refer to people who must have every new technological gadget produced by the denizens of the Silicon Valley. But neophilia is not limited to the world of technological gadgetry. It also extends to the realm of ideas. Many people in our culture are philosophical neophiliacs who eschew tradition and history in favor of embracing every new idea they encounter. These philosophical neophiliacs employ buzzwords such as *change* and *progress* to describe their ethos. For the neophiliac, history and tradition are viewed with disdain. Like Ford, the philosophical neophile cries out: "We don't want tradition. We want to live in the present, and the only history that is worth a tinker's damn is the history that we make today."

In this chapter, we will explore how neophilia is at odds with a God-centered worldview. We'll see that the Bible teaches us to love, respect, honor, and preserve tradition. We'll also see how our adversary seeks to gain an advantage by loosing us from the moorings of tradition and history. We'll see the great damage caused by neophilia in education, the church, and the culture at large.

The Biblical Worldview: Preservation Trumps Progress

The book of Proverbs is a collection of divinely inspired wisdom that God gave to his covenant people to guide them in living a godly and blessed life in this age. Among the many admonishments found in this book is the following: "Do not

move an ancient boundary stone set up by your forefathers"
(Prov. 22:28).

This admonishment from Proverbs informs us that there
are two types of people in this world: the fool who relishes in
moving boundary stones (a "stone mover") and the wise who
endeavors to preserve boundary stones (a "stone preserver").

Stone movers are essentially transformationalists at heart.
They are driven by the conviction that the stones are in the
wrong place, that the forefathers spoken of in Proverbs 22:28
simply erred. Generally, stone movers come to this conclusion
because they think themselves more enlightened and freer
from prejudice than their forefathers. They come to believe that
it is their duty to move the boundary stones. They feel com-
pelled to convince others of this same conclusion, to remove
the veil before their eyes and to disavow them of their ancient
prejudices. They see themselves not as stewards of a sacred
trust, but rather as pioneers on a crusade. Their ethos is not
fiduciary in nature, but rather revolutionary.

Charles Bridges accurately described the attitude of stone
movers in his comments on Proverbs 22:28: "Some scorn *the
ancient landmarks* as relics of bye-gone days of darkness. Impa-
tient of restraint, they want a wider range of wandering to
indulge their own prurient appetite for novelties, or the morbid
cravings of others for this unwholesome excitement."[3] Stone
movers have a voracious "appetite for novelties"; they love all
things new. They are enamored of the prospect of rejecting
the past and transforming the current order.

In contrast, stone preservers are essentially preservation-
ists at heart. They believe that the stones are in the right place
and must be protected at all costs. They desire to be good
stewards of what has been entrusted to them. They feel driven
to convince others that the stones are in the right place, and

---

3. Charles Bridges, *Proverbs* (Carlisle, PA: Banner of Truth, 1998), 422 (emphasis
in original).

they have a disdain for revolutionaries. Their greatest fear is that any movement of the stones will upset the social order and lead to chaos. The Puritan Matthew Henry aptly reflects the disposition of the stone preservers in his comments on Proverbs 22:28: "We may infer hence that a deference is to be paid, in all civil matters, to usages that have prevailed time out of mind and the settled constitutions of government, in which it becomes us to acquiesce, lest an attempt to change it, under pretence of changing it for the better, prove of dangerous consequence."[4] Stone preservers are inclined to defend at all costs the "usages that have prevailed time out of mind." They are enraptured with the hope of preserving a traditional order, of preserving the boundary stones. They believe the old way should be preserved unless it is clearly shown to be wrong.

The Bible calls Christians to the task of being stone preservers. This is made clear not only in Proverbs, but throughout the Bible. We see it made manifest in the garden of Eden, in the life of Israel, in the fifth commandment, and in the apostolic church. According to God's Word, the bias is in favor of the old over the new. In the Bible, preservation trumps progress.

Take Care of the Garden

The first place where we witness a call for preservation is in the garden of Eden. After God created a good and perfect world, he then created an upright moral creature to dwell in it. God placed man in his perfect garden and gave him two tasks that are recorded in Genesis 2:15: "The LORD God took the man and put him in the Garden of Eden *to work it and take care of it.*" Adam was called to be the steward of God's good world by working it and guarding it. As God's priest, Adam was commissioned with the task of guarding the garden from outside evil forces seeking to spoil and profane it. The phrase

4. Matthew Henry, *Matthew Henry's Commentary on the Whole Bible*, vol. 3 (Peabody, MA: Hendrickson, 1991), 758.

"take care of it" specifically refers to this priestly calling.[5] Adam was called to keep and preserve the good.

Of course, Adam failed in this commission. He became enamored of his own glory and abilities and sought to improve the good world that God had given to him. After all, wouldn't the world be a better place if he had the knowledge of good and evil? Wouldn't the possession of this forbidden knowledge represent progress for humanity? God did not view Adam's disobedience as progress, but rather only as disobedience. In his search for human improvement, Adam had lost his priestly calling. He was escorted east of Eden, and God replaced him with cherubim, who were now charged with the task of preserving the garden from the profane and unholy, including the unholy Adam (Gen. 3:24). In the garden, preservation trumped progress.

Avoid Addition and Subtraction

Another place where we witness a call for preservation is in the book of Deuteronomy. In Deuteronomy, Moses assumed the role of Israel's teacher. He passed on to the children of Israel the commands that he had received directly from the hand and mouth of God. But before he began his instruction, Moses prefaced his teaching with this singular command: "Do not add to what I command you and do not subtract from it, but keep the commands of the LORD your God that I give you" (Deut. 4:2).[6]

Moses commanded God's people to avoid engaging in addition and subtraction when it came to God's revelation and commands. Just as Adam was called to keep God's holy

5. It is important to remember that the garden functioned as God's holy temple and that Adam's tasks within it were priestly in nature and not agricultural. As J. V. Fesko so aptly puts it, "Adam was an archetypal priest, not a farmer." J. V. Fesko, *First Things Last* (Fearn, Ross-shire, UK: Mentor, 2007), 75.

6. A similar command appears at the very end of God's Word: "And if anyone takes words away from this book of prophecy, God will take away from him his share in the tree of life and in the holy city, which are described in this book" (Rev. 22:19).

garden, Moses called Israel to "keep" God's holy law. Israel was forbidden from engaging in vain efforts to improve God's perfect word. In the book of Deuteronomy, preservation trumped progress.

The Faith Once Entrusted

The call for preservation is not just an Old Testament concept. We also encounter this call in the context of the New Testament. The apostles viewed themselves as those entrusted with the teachings of the Lord Jesus Christ. They had been commissioned by King Jesus with the task of teaching the world everything that Jesus had commanded. Like Adam and Israel before them, the apostles were called to the task of preservation.

We see an example of the apostles' commitment to this task in Paul's instruction regarding the Lord's Supper in 1 Corinthians 11:23: "*For I received from the Lord what I also passed on to you*: The Lord Jesus, on the night he was betrayed, took bread." Paul was careful to preface his instructions with a statement demonstrating that he was simply passing on the teaching of the Lord Jesus.

Jude also reflects the spirit of apostolic preservation in the opening verses of his epistle, but he extends this task to the entire church: "Dear friends, although I was very eager to write to you about the salvation we share, I felt I had to write and *urge you to contend for the faith that was once for all entrusted to the saints*" (Jude 3). Jude reminds the saints of this congregation that the task of the church is preserving, not altering, the "faith that was once for all entrusted to the saints." In the New Testament, preservation trumped progress.

These three examples demonstrate the biblical bias toward preserving what has gone before. God called Adam, Israel, and the New Israel to the task of stewarding a history and tradition. He called them to preserve the good and protect it from the corrupting influences of outside evil, be it in the form of a serpent, our own sinful hearts, or false teachers. This calling continues for Christians today. It means that as Christians we must be conservationists of God's holy Word and his created order.

To perform this calling, we must learn, know, remember, preserve, and respect history. It is not a mere coincidence that the Jews were among the first of the cultures to excel as historians and to view history in a linear fashion. As "people of the Book," Christians are in essence a historical people called to remember and preserve the ways of God because the Bible teaches us that preservation trumps progress.

The Worldview of the Adversary: Progress Trumps Preservation

In contrast to the biblical worldview that stresses preservation over progress, the worldview of our adversary stresses exactly the opposite. From the very beginning, Satan has attempted to alter God's created order by introducing a new one—his own alternative order. Satan has continually enlisted human agents and nations to initiate his wicked agenda. His strategy involves enticing humanity to follow him rather than God, and one of the ways he achieves this is by dressing up his evil agenda in the appealing garb of the "new." Like a Madison Avenue advertising executive, Satan is continually trying to seduce us with a worldview system that he touts as "new and improved." Our adversary encourages us to ignore what has gone before, to forget history and tradition, and to engage in a never-ending pursuit of tomorrow. Satan is the ultimate neophiliac, and he wants all of us to join him in his neophilia. According to the worldview of the adversary, the new is always better than the old—progress always trumps preservation.

When we survey the landscape of our world, we are forced to conclude that Satan has waged a very successful campaign against the past. Neophilia is rampant in our age. Tradition and history are viewed as suspect, while newness is embraced with religious fervor. Our adversary is winning victories by convincing our age to genuflect before the idol of progress. The spirit of neophilia prevails in our culture, in the sphere of education, and even in the church.

The People of Progress

One of the marks of the modern age is a fascination with the future. Modern man's pride is centered in his perceived progress. The modernist viewed the past with disdain and considered it irrelevant to the ever-unfolding future. This modernist spirit is vividly displayed in F. T. Marinetti's *Futurist Manifesto*, written in 1909. Among Marinetti's admonitions to the people of the newly born twentieth century was the following: "We are on the extreme promontory of the centuries! What is the use of looking behind at the moment when we must open the mysterious shutters of the impossible? Time and Space died yesterday. We are already living in the absolute, since we have already created eternal, omnipresent speed."[7] For the modernist, there was no use looking back to yesterday; the only thing that mattered was looking through the "mysterious shutters of the impossible" and "living in the absolute" of the present moment.

As the twentieth century matured, the tenets of modernity, including its wholesale rejection of the past, came under assault. Modernism had given way to postmodernism. Unlike modernism, postmodernism is interested in the past, but not in a way that agrees with the biblical worldview on history. Let me explain by way of a metaphor.

One of the metaphors used to describe our postmodern age is the collage or pastiche. In such a view, many dispa-

7. F. T. Marinetti, "The Futurist Manifesto," in *Intellectuals in Politics: Three Biographical Essays*, trans. James Joll (London: Weidenfeld & Nicolson, 1960), available at cscs.umich.edu/~crshalizi/T4PM/futurist-manifesto.html.

rate, and often incompatible, elements are joined together. The postmodernist is interested in incorporating into his collage of reality elements of both the past and the present. So postmoderns do explore and study the past, but they do so only to relativize it to this contemporary moment. In other words, postmoderns seek to make history contemporary. Gene Veith explains the postmodernist view of history: "Postmodernism thus has history, but not a 'sense of history,' since all historical moments are reduced, swallowed up by the contemporary, and relativized."[8] Veith concludes that while postmodernism's openness to history is valuable, its use of history results in a "schizoid pastiche" that values only the "perpetual present."[9]

The views of history espoused by modernism and postmodernism have found root throughout our culture. These are not merely intellectual ideas relegated to the ivory tower of academia. They are made manifest in the daily lives of people. People in our age covet the contemporary; they desire the new—the new car, the new technological device, or the new church. The past is worthy only to the extent that it can be incorporated into the moment in which we live. In our day, progress trumps preservation.

The danger of this infatuation with newness and progress is that it inevitably entails a rejection of God's sovereignty over history and an acceptance of the unbounded abilities of humanity. Christopher Lasch noted that the progressive optimism of our culture "rests, at bottom, on a denial of the natural limits on human power and freedom."[10] In the end, our cultural fascination with progress is simply another reenactment of the Tower of Babel, where prideful humanity exhibited a "denial of the natural limits on human power and freedom." By rejecting the past and embracing progress, we

8. Gene E. Veith Jr., *Postmodern Times* (Wheaton, IL: Crossway, 1994), 100.
9. Ibid., 99.
10. Christopher Lasch, *The True and Only Heaven: Progress and Its Critics* (New York: W. W. Norton & Company, 1991), 530.

are ultimately rejecting God and embracing the idol of ourselves. This is exactly what Satan desires us to do.

In our world, progress and newness are part and parcel of our cultural expectation and religion. Politicians promise "change" because they know it is the idol of our age. Christopher Dawson was correct when he noted that progress is the "working faith of our civilization."[11] We are the people who live in the absolute of the "perpetual present." We are the people who are ignorant of the past. We are the people of progress.

The Professors of Progress

A second area in which neophilia has had a profound negative impact is in the realm of education. From the perspective of a biblical worldview, education is an act of preservation and conveyance. The educator is to convey to the student God's revealed truth, be it revealed through God's Word or through God's world. As Cornelius Van Til put it, the goal of education is to "think God's thoughts after him."[12] Inherent in Van Til's definition is the idea that education is a historical undertaking in which man endeavors to think God's thoughts after him. True education is anchored by the knowledge and recognition of the Creator: "The fear of the LORD is the beginning of knowledge, but fools despise wisdom and discipline" (Prov. 1:7). Therefore, the goal of education and educators should be to preserve and convey God's truth.

Many educators, particularly those serving in public and higher education, do not see their task as one of preservation and conveyance. Rather, they consider themselves entrusted with the task of deconstructing a biblical worldview and erecting in its place the new edifice of secular humanism. For them, education is not about preservation, but rather about progress.

---

11. Quoted in ibid., 43.
12. Cornelius Van Til, "The Education of Man—A Divinely Ordained Need," *Fundamentals In Christian Education*, ed. Cornelius Jaarsma (Eerdmans: Grand Rapids, MI, 1953), 40.

And to them, progress involves eviscerating the fear of the Lord from the pursuit of knowledge.

The neophilia that runs rampant in modern education is a powerful tool in the hands of our adversary because it involves our children. Just as a lion searches through a herd of antelope for the youngest among the herd, so our adversary seeks to prey on our children. Dinesh D'Souza notes the power of this wicked but effective strategy:

> It seems that atheists are not content with committing cultural suicide—they want to take your children with them. The atheist strategy can be described in this way: let the religious people breed them, and we will educate them to despise their parents' beliefs. So the secularization of the minds of our young people is not, as many think, the inevitable consequence of learning and maturing. Rather, it is to a large degree orchestrated by teachers and professors to promote anti-religious agendas.[13]

For the professors of progress, indoctrinating our children with the knowledge of God is an act akin to child abuse.[14] They see it as their job to replace the knowledge of God with the new and improved wisdom of this world. Accordingly, the professors of progress replace creation with chaos, sexual discretion with sexual tolerance, and true freedom of God's law with the chains of man's autonomy.

The Pastors and Parishioners of Progress

The church has not been immune to the pernicious power of unbridled neophilia. The church also seems to have an insatiable passion for the new. The church in our day is not

13. Dinesh D'Souza, *What's So Great about Christianity?* (Carol Stream, IL: Tyndale House, 2007), 33.

14. For example, Richard Dawkins writes, "Isn't it always a form of child abuse to label children as possessors of beliefs that they are too young to have thought about?" Richard Dawkins, *The God Delusion* (Boston: Houghton Mifflin, 2006), 315.

enamored of the faith once entrusted to the saints; rather, it is more interested in being culturally relevant and genuine. Nowhere can the present power of neophilia be seen more clearly than in the emerging-church movement.

What is the emerging-church movement? By design, it is terribly difficult to pin down an exact definition, but D. A. Carson provides us with some guidance:

> At the heart of the "movement"—or as some of its leaders prefer to call it, the "conversation"—lies the conviction that changes in the culture signal that a new church is "emerging." Christian leaders must therefore adapt to this emerging church. Those who fail to do so are blind to the cultural accretions that hide the gospel behind forms of thought and modes of expression that no longer communicate with the new generation, the emerging generation.[15]

The emerging church emphasizes tolerance and pluralism. It abhors confident statements of certainty, even when they are drawn from the Bible. Subjective personal experiences, rather than objective propositions, are viewed as the best means of arriving at and articulating truth. In the end, the emerging church rejects the biblical principle of preserving the faith once delivered to the saints. D. A. Carson has criticized the emerging-church movement because it results in an "almost universal condemnation of confessional Christianity."[16] The emerging-church movement is simply a baptized version of our wider culture's insatiable quest to live in the "perpetual present." It is offering what it believes is a new and improved version of Christianity.

Who is leading this emerging-church movement? A new generation of theological leaders who are eager to drag the

15. D. A. Carson, *Becoming Conversant with the Emerging Church* (Grand Rapids: Zondervan, 2005), 12.
16. Ibid., 64.

church into the waters of the postmodern world. They are the pastors of progress. They are educated, stylish, hip, techno-savvy, and, of course, relevant. They are, at heart, innovators seeking to engage in a protest against the traditional church and its understanding of Scripture and truth. David Wells wrote the following about Brian McLaren, one of the major pastoral leaders of this movement: "McLaren thinks historic faith needs to be de-reconstructed for postmoderns so that the baggage of enduring truth can be dropped."[17]

But it's not just the pastoral leaders of the emerging church who have given in to the cultural thirst for the contemporary; this spirit is present throughout evangelicalism. In his book *The Courage to Be Protestant*, David Wells points out how over the past thirty years evangelicals have "discovered culture." Wells goes on to note that this discovery of culture has not led to a sufficient critique of it by evangelicals, but rather a wholesale embracing of it. Evangelicals have brought the culture into the church. Wells writes of evangelicals:

> What they want to know about culture is simple and easy to unearth. They want to know what the trends and fashions are that are ruffling the surface of contemporary life. They have no interest at all in what lies beneath the trends, none on how our modernized culture in the West shapes personal horizons, produces appetites, and provides us ways of process-ing the meaning of life. All of that seems like pretty complex and useless stuff. Pragmatists to the last drop of blood, these evangelicals are now in the cultural waters, not to understand what is there, but to get some movement.[18]

The evangelical church has immersed itself in the cultural quest for progress, and what has been lost in the wake of this

17. David Wells, *The Courage to Be Protestant* (Grand Rapids: Eerdmans, 2008), 87.
18. Ibid., 3. Wells is perhaps painting with too broad a brush here, since there are some lively critiques of culture within certain evangelical circles.

quest is sound biblical doctrine and reverent biblical worship. The pastors of progress, dressed in the garb of marketers and entrepreneurs, have bulldozed tradition and confessional Christianity in order to build the icon of twenty-first-century evangelicalism: the megachurch. As Os Guinness has noted, much of modern evangelicalism has built the church on *sola cultura* instead of *sola Scriptura*.[19]

Are New Ideas Always Bad?

In this chapter, I have illustrated the negative effects of an unbridled passion for new things in the culture, in education, and in the church. I have argued that the Bible supports an attitude of preservation over progress. But this raises the question, "Are new ideas always bad?" The answer to that question is an emphatic, but qualified, "no!" Let me explain.

New ideas *are* always bad when they involve moving away from a God-centered biblical worldview. But sometimes ideas we refer to as new actually move us away from sin and closer to God, and when this is true, we should embrace these "new" ideas. Take, for example, the historical pattern of racism in America. The civil-rights movement represented a new idea for America, but it was an idea that was entirely in accord with a God-centered worldview. The great civil-rights leader Dr. Martin Luther King Jr. understood that the persuasive argument for equality is found in a biblical worldview. Another example of change and newness producing great good was the Reformation. The Reformation represented a break with the tradition that had preceded it, yet this break was one that drew the church closer to a God-centered worldview.

But what is important to see in the examples of the civil-rights movement and the Reformation is that the ideas embraced in them were not really new. Both of these move-

---

19. Os Guinness, *Prophetic Untimeliness: A Challenge to the Idol of Relevance* (Baker: Grand Rapids, MI, 2003), 65.

ments were recovering the truth of the Bible, not manufacturing it. This reminds us of an important caveat when it comes to analyzing the traditions of our culture. Because of the sinful nature of humanity, some of our social boundary stones do not reflect the order of the Creator, but rather the order of fallen humanity. Of course, the challenge resides in determining which boundary stones are reflective of fallen humanity and which are reflective of the Creator's eternal principles.[20] This challenge is complex and difficult, but it is the task of Christians to engage the challenge with a discerning mind.

Preserve the Permanent Things and Protect the Shire

It is vitally important for Christians to grasp that a central component of our adversary's strategy is to make the world fall madly in love with this present age. Satan achieves victory when people forget the past and ignore the future. Satan desires to convince us to focus on this age because he is the "god of this age" (2 Cor. 4:4). Satan seeks to usurp God's kingly rule, and one way he achieves this end is by convincing the world to live only in the now and in the new.

Over the past several centuries, secularism has been the fastest-growing religion in the world. Secularism promotes a rejection of God and a rejection of the past. While secularists take pride in the supposed worldly intellectual sophistication of their view, G. K. Chesterton had it right when he noted that *secular* "does not mean anything so sensible as 'worldly.' It does not even mean anything so spirited as 'irreligious.' To be secular simply means to be of the age; that is, of the age which is passing."[21]

The worldview of secular neophilia is at war with the worldview of the Bible. Christians can resist the temptations of secular neophilia by endeavoring to preserve what T. S. Eliot

---

20. Sean Michael Lewis describes the tension of this problem as it was displayed in the lives and thought of Abraham Kuyper and Robert Lewis Dabney. Sean Michael Lewis, "Southern-Fried Kuyper? Robert Lewis Dabney, Abraham Kuyper, and the Limitations of Public Theology," *Westminster Theological Journal* 66 (Spring 2004): 179–201.

21. G. K. Chesterton, *Collected Works* (San Francisco: Ignatius Press, 1986), 3:388–89.

referred to as the "permanent things."[22] The permanent things are those enduring aspects of God's created order that are worthy of defense and are rooted in a Christian worldview. Preserving these aspects means that we resist worshiping the "god of this age" and instead worship the "Rock of Ages." It means that we honor our fathers and mothers and the great cloud of witnesses that surround us by fostering what G. K. Chesterton referred to as the "democracy of the dead":

> Tradition means giving voices to the most obscure of all classes, our ancestors. It is the democracy of the dead. Tradition refuses to submit to the small and arrogant oligarchy of those who merely happen to be walking about. All democrats object to men being disqualified by the accident of birth; tradition objects to their being disqualified by the accident of death. Democracy tells us not to neglect a good man's opinion, even if he is our groom; tradition asks us not to neglect a good man's opinion, even if he is our father.[23]

Chesterton was calling us all to extend equal voting rights to the past.

In practical terms, this means that in the face of a culture infatuated with the "new," we should stand firm for the "old" biblical definitions of marriage, family, and freedom. It means that we need to counter the worldview of secular education by endeavoring to educate our children in the fear of the Lord and in the knowledge of their Creator. Finally, it means that we must fight a tireless counterinsurgency against the pastors of progress by defending the faith once entrusted to the saints. Instead of embracing the new emerging-church trends, we must embrace the old creeds and confessions of the church.

22. T.S. Eliot, *Christianity & Culture: The Idea of a Christian Society and Notes Towards the Definition of Culture* (New York: Harcourt, Brace, 1940), 102.
23. Chesterton, *Collected Works*, 1:251.

In J. R. R. Tolkien's grand tale *The Lord of the Rings*, Frodo and his fellow hobbits are on a mission of preserving a way of life: life in the Shire. It is the evil servants of Mordor who endeavor to bring change, progress, and newness through machines, genetic mutation, and the tearing down of the existing world order. In telling his tale in these terms, Tolkien was defending a biblical perspective on the world. He was calling his readers to preserve the permanent things. The Bible calls us to engage in exactly the same task. As Christians, we are called to preserve the Shire of God's created order against the neophilia of the adversary.

4

Egalitarianism

"We're All in Charge"

The propaganda of egalitarianism encourages belief that any society embodying distinctions must necessarily be torn with envy and hatred.
—Richard M. Weaver[1]

THE DECLARATION OF INDEPENDENCE asserts that "all men are created equal." These words have been interpreted in two ways. Some view these words as a declaration that all men have equal rights under the law and should be free to pursue life, liberty, and happiness according to their abilities. Others view these words in a different manner. They see them as a broad statement of equality that promises not just equality before the law, but also equality in privileges, abilities, and outcomes. This latter view is known as egalitarianism.

Egalitarians genuflect before the idol of equality. For them, equality is all that matters, even if equality must be enforced

1. Richard M. Weaver, *Visions of Order* (Bryn Mawr, PA: Intercollegiate Studies Institute, 1995).

by the iron fist of the state. Egalitarians despise authority that flows from hierarchy. They endeavor to bring a leveling to all hierarchies. According to egalitarians, people should not be ruled over by elites who have superior skills, abilities, and intellect. Instead, they believe we should all be equally involved in governing ourselves. The egalitarian believes that we are all equal and we are all in charge.

In this chapter, we will explore how the principles of egalitarianism run contrary to a God-centered worldview. We will see that while the Bible teaches us that we are all created equal, it does not teach us that we are all equal with respect to privileges, abilities, and outcomes. We will also see how our adversary uses the spirit of egalitarianism to undermine order in our world and in the church.

The Biblical Worldview: Hierarchy and Order

God hates chaos and disorder. He is a God of order, and the Bible clearly represents this divine bias toward order. The Bible also reveals that God establishes this order through a form of inequality. Order in the Bible is achieved by means of hierarchy.

Hierarchy involves a system in which there are superiors and subordinates. In a properly established hierarchy, the superiors in the system achieve their status because they possess superior qualities as the result of their natural abilities and experience. Such a hierarchy produces peace and order because the most qualified people are in charge. The Bible is hierarchical from beginning to end. According to the biblical worldview, hierarchy and order are more important than equality. We see this principle in various places throughout the Bible.

Hierarchy in the Creation of the World

We all know that God created the world in six days. But what is less well known is the fact that these six days reflect God's propensity for establishing systems of order and hierarchy. As many scholars have recognized, the six days of creation are composed of two triads of days. The first three days compose the first triad, and days four through six compose the second triad. The following is a diagram of these two triads:[2]

FIRST TRIAD	SECOND TRIAD
Day One: Light—Genesis 1:3–5	**Day Four:** Lights—Genesis 1:14–19
Day Two: Firmament (sky & seas)—Genesis 1:6–8	**Day Five:** Inhabitants (birds & fish)—Genesis 1:20–23
Day Three: Dry land—Genesis 1:9–10 Vegetation—Genesis 1:11–13	**Day Six:** Land animals—Genesis 1:24–25 Human beings—Genesis 1:26–31

In the creation, God brought order to the universe by creating different spheres: light, firmament, and dry land. He then filled these various spheres with inhabitants: lights, birds, fish, land animals, and human beings. But God's order is not only witnessed in this sphere/filling-of-sphere pattern, but also witnessed in the hierarchy that the Creator establishes within each sphere. According to the Bible, the inhabitants created in the second triad of days "rule" over the sphere created in the first triad of days. Consider the following examples of this hierarchical pattern from Genesis:

Lights: "God made two great lights—the greater light *to govern* the day and the lesser light *to govern* the night" (Gen. 1:16).

Humans: "Then God said, 'Let us make man in our image, in our likeness, and let them *rule over* the fish of the sea and

2. This chart is adapted from Bruce Waltke, *Genesis* (Grand Rapids: Zondervan, 2001), 57.

the birds of the air, over the livestock, over all the earth, and over all the creatures that move along the ground'" (Gen. 1:26).

When God created the world, he displayed his preference for order achieved through hierarchy. He created a world with superiors and inferiors. He created a world of hierarchy, not equality.

Hierarchy in the Creation of Man

When one reads of the creation of man in Genesis 1:26, it is clear that mankind has been placed at the top of the hierarchy of created beings. Mankind was created with dominion of the creation and all its inhabitants. But it is a dreadful mistake to conclude from this truth that mankind is free to exercise his dominion in any way he chooses. Mankind also has a superior. Man is merely a vice-regent who serves the true King of this world. God's pattern of hierarchy is also revealed in his creation of man.

First, hierarchy is evident in the creation of man by the mere fact that man is created by God. Man is not self-existent like God; rather, he is a created being. God is the Creator and man is the creature. This Creator-creature distinction is one of the most basic principles of sound theology.

A second way in which hierarchy manifests itself in the creation of man is seen in what God does with man after creating him. Genesis tells us that God demonstrated his superiority and dominion over man by placing him in a garden and dictating the terms of their covenant relationship. God told Adam that this enjoyment of life in the garden with God was dependent on his perfect obedience to God's law.

The creation of man demonstrates that there is a fundamental and unalterable hierarchical order in this world. Man may be the pinnacle of God's creative work, but he by no means arrives at equality with God. God has no equal, and man has no right to autonomous rule. God created a world of hierarchy, not equality.

Hierarchy in the Church

God's pattern of establishing hierarchical order may also be witnessed in his church. In both the Old Testament and the New Testament, God set forth principles for his church to be governed in a hierarchical paradigm. The Scriptures make it clear that the church is not an egalitarian institution.

Although there is some debate among scholars, the general consensus is that the church began with Abraham. When God established his church, he did it by choosing a patriarch to be its earthly ruler. Abraham was given the covenant. Abraham was instructed, as the chief priest of the church, to administer the sacrament of circumcision.

From the time of Abraham to the exile in Egypt, the church was governed by the descendants of Abraham. In the time of the exodus, God chose Moses to lead his church. It was through Moses that God performed his signs and wonders. Moses was the mediator of God's covenant. Moses delivered the Ten Commandments to the people. When Korah rebelled against Moses and attempted to institute his own form of egalitarianism in Israel, God responded with swift judgment against the insolent rebels (Num. 16). During the time of Moses, God expanded the hierarchical order of his church by providing Moses with seventy elders to assist in the governance of the people (Num. 11).

After the exodus, the Old Testament church was ruled primarily by judges and the prophet Samuel. Eventually, Israel desired a king to replace the system of judges. Then, during the rule of David, the Old Testament church was governed through a three-office hierarchy of prophets, priests, and kings. The order in these offices was not to be confused or undermined, even by other officeholders, as is indicated by the fate of King Uzziah. In his pride, King Uzziah attempted to usurp the role of the priests by burning incense in the temple, and God struck him with leprosy (2 Chron. 26:16–23).

When one surveys the history and structure of the Old Testament church, it is abundantly clear that God ordered his church in a hierarchical fashion. Just as he did in the days of creation, God set forth a pattern of order and rule in his church with clearly delineated boundaries of authority that were not to be crossed or confused. God brought swift judgment against those who violated this order or subverted this hierarchical structure. This hierarchical pattern did not end with the close of the Old Testament, but continued in the New Testament church.

The continuity of hierarchical governance of the church is made clear in the early parts of Jesus' public ministry. One of the first actions Jesus takes is the calling of the twelve apostles. Just as Israel had twelve tribes led by twelve patriarchs, the New Israel would have twelve leaders. Jesus had a unique relationship with these twelve men. He exclusively taught them the mysteries of his kingdom (Matt. 13:11). He gave them the keys of the kingdom (16:19) and the Great Commission (28:18–20).

The book of Acts reveals that the church was governed in a hierarchical structure, with the apostles at the top of the hierarchy. Acts 15 presents us with a portrait of an early church court composed of the elders of the church and presided over by the apostle James. A bit earlier in the book of Acts, we see another parallel to the Old Testament church as Paul establishes elders as rulers of local congregations (Acts 14:23). When Paul was approaching the end of his life and ministry, he commissioned the elders of the church to continue the ministry by serving as shepherds and overseers of the church (20:17–38).

The New Testament Epistles, particularly the Pastoral Epistles (1 Timothy, 2 Timothy, and Titus), reveal a well-defined series of church offices, including pastor, elder, and deacon.

The epistle to the Hebrews admonishes the people of the congregation to respect the ruling authority of the leadership of the church: "Obey your leaders and submit to their authority. They keep watch over you as men who must give an account. Obey them so that their work will be a joy, not a burden, for that would be of no advantage to you" (Heb. 13:17).

A survey of the New Testament also reveals that God established a hierarchy in his church. The church is not a democracy. Even in the book of Revelation, which portrays in symbolic terms the order of heaven, we see the Lamb on the throne and around him are twenty-four elders (Rev. 4:4). Heaven is a hierarchy.

The creation of the world, the creation of man, and the governance of the church all reveal a distinct pattern in which God establishes order through hierarchy. While all Christians are equal in the sense that they are created in the image of God (Gen. 1:26) and redeemed by Christ (Gal. 3:28), this does not mean that this equality extends to all aspects of the Christian life and God's created order. Biblical egalitarianism is limited to equality in being; it does not extend to equality in outcome, governance, and authority. When it comes to how Christians are to relate in society, the home, and the church, the biblical worldview stresses hierarchy and order over egalitarianism and autonomy.

The Worldview of the Adversary: Equality and Autonomy

In opposition to the biblical worldview, our adversary promotes a worldview that seeks to undermine God's created order of hierarchy and order. Satan achieves this by appealing to our self-love and inherent pride. Satan knows the power of these forces very well because his own origins involved a prideful desire to undermine God's set patterns of hierarchy and to institute his own form of equality and autonomy. Satan emerged as an adversary to God and his people by desiring to make himself like "the Most High" (Isa. 14:14).

The fall of mankind reveals that human nature has an innate inclination toward rebelling against God's hierarchical rule and created order. Like Satan, Adam and Eve desired to establish an egalitarian society in which they became like God (Gen. 3:5). This human propensity toward self-love and self-rule makes us easy prey for Satan. We are naturally inclined to adopt the worldview of our adversary. When we do, it causes great damage in both our culture and the church.

The Destructive Effects of Egalitarianism in Our Culture

Democracy is a great idea. It provides for equality of all people before the law and in the political process. But democracy can be a terribly destructive idea when it becomes a transcendent concept applied to all spheres of human experience. As Richard Weaver noted, "When democracy is taken from its proper place and is allowed to fill the entire horizon, it produces an envious hatred not only of all distinction but even of all difference."[3] When the egalitarian spirit of democracy permeates an entire culture, the consequences include simple silliness, perverted populism, and absolute autonomy.

The idea of egalitarianism has so saturated our culture that it has trickled down even to the level of our children. Ours is the age in which no child is left behind and everybody wins. Any distinctions regarding the ability or outcomes of children are viewed as being unfair, discriminatory, and unjust. We live in a culture in which everyone gets a trophy. This effort to bring outcome egalitarianism to education and children's sports is silly, deceitful, and ultimately harmful to children and our culture. Much has been written about the sense of entitlement among Millennials (aka Generation Y, those born between 1981 and 1994) and how this is affecting their experi-

3. Richard M. Weaver, *Visions of Order* (Bryn Mawr, PA: Intercollegiate Studies Institute, 1995), 15.

ences in higher education and the workforce.[4] One example of the type of silliness created by this egalitarian spirit is an anecdote from a human resources director who recounts how an employee's mother called to complain that her daughter received a poor performance review![5] The widespread adoption of outcome egalitarianism is contributing to a culture of entitlement in which self-centered adolescence is prolonged into adulthood. We are raising a generation of children who have been deceived by the lie that we all deserve a trophy.

Egalitarianism is also having a destructive impact in the realm of politics and social debate. The spirit of egalitarianism has given rise to the idea that every person's opinion is of equal value regardless of his or her qualifications. Egalitarianism casts a skeptical eye at any notion of elitism or hierarchy. It balks at the idea that perhaps some people are more qualified to speak to certain issues than others. Egalitarianism prefers the common sense of the laymen to the educated assessment of the studied elite. This egalitarian spirit has resulted in a form of anti-intellectual populism that has eroded the quality of civic debate in our culture.

In our culture today, the egalitarian idea that everyone is equally capable of rendering a valid opinion on complex matters is pervasive. Two recent media developments have taken this type of egalitarian notion to new levels. The first was the growth of talk radio and the second the introduction of the Internet, particularly the phenomenon of blogging. These mediums encourage the emotive display of shared ignorance in which every man's opinion is regarded as equal in value. The end result is a culture that is less civil in its discourse and less reasoned in its analysis. It drags down the entire level of public discourse as politicians and television talking heads

4. One example is Bruce Tulgan's *Not Everyone Gets a Trophy: How to Manage Generation Y* (San Francisco: Jossey-Bass, 2009).

5. Bill Redeker, "Meet the New Millennials: They're Young, Cool and Not Keen to Get to Work Before 10 a.m.," May 18, 2007, www.abcnews.go.com.

cater to the lowest common denominator. We have exchanged the ideal of Plato's philosopher-kings for the likes of Rush Limbaugh and Keith Olbermann.

In the end, our culture's widespread embracing of egalitarianism is having profoundly negative effects in our society. It deceives our children and leaves them unprepared for the real world. It erodes the quality of public debate and undermines civic discourse. It fosters envy, hatred, and suspicion. Ultimately, egalitarianism encourages a sense of personal autonomy and entitlement that subverts the order and effectiveness of our society.

The Destructive Effects of Egalitarianism in the Church

The church is often like a sponge that absorbs the spirit of the age prevalent in the surrounding culture. This is certainly the case with the dangerous idea of egalitarianism. The church has drunk deeply from the culture's egalitarian well, and it is hobbling the church's work and ministry. As with the rise of egalitarianism in American culture, we can trace the roots of the rise of ecclesiastical egalitarianism back to the Great Awakening of the mid-eighteenth century.

One of the marks of the Great Awakening was the rejection of the idea of an educated clergy.[6] Anti-intellectualism was on the rise within the rank and file of the church. A minister who possessed a seminary education was viewed with suspicion. The trained leadership was rejected in favor of the theology and rule of the average man. This theological egalitarianism was bolstered by the Second Great Awakening (1790–1840).

Modern evangelicalism can trace its lineage back to the Second Great Awakening, and so it should not come as a surprise that evangelicalism is dominated by an egalitarian ethos. Evangelicalism has given us the independent church, which rejects all outside authority and hierarchy and instead

6. Richard Hofstadter, *Anti-Intellectualism in American Life* (New York: Vintage Books, 1963), 64.

embraces democratic self-rule. Evangelicalism has rejected the historical creeds and confessions in favor of the theological fancies of the untrained pastor of the moment. Evangelicalism has disrobed and demoted the clergy, choosing instead to invest ecclesiastical authority in the laity based on a perverse misunderstanding of the Reformation doctrine of the priesthood of all believers. In the evangelical church, everyone is in charge. The person in the pew is an empowered consumer exercising free choice in the governance of the church. In evangelicalism, it is all about me and my Bible.

But this ecclesiastical egalitarianism is not just confined to the ranks of superficial evangelicalism. It is also rife within the Reformed world. For example, R. Scott Clark argues in his book *Recovering the Reformed Confession* that many in the Reformed church have "spurned the objective reality of the Reformed confession in favor of their own reflection."[7] This theological egalitarianism is present both in the pew and in the pulpit. Truth and authority is not found in the historical teachings of the church, but rather in the private interpretation of each person. Clark writes, "It seems widely assumed today that whatever one understands Scripture to teach or imply must *ipso facto* be Reformed. The reasoning seems to be thus: I am Reformed, I think *p*, and therefore *p* must be Reformed."[8] As Clark so aptly puts it, we live in the age of "Narcissus Reformed."[9]

The destructive effects of the pervasiveness of egalitarianism in the church are manifold. First, ecclesiastical egalitarianism undermines the objective truth and authority of Scripture by rendering it subservient to individual interpretation and experience. Second, this mind-set eviscerates the authority of the prophetic and ruling functions of the church. The pastor's proclamation of the Word is viewed as just another man's

7. R. Scott Clark, *Recovering the Reformed Confession* (Phillipsburg, NJ: P&R Publishing, 2008), 17.
8. Ibid., 18.
9. Ibid., 31.

opinion, and the elders' attempts at exercising discipline over the flock are viewed as wholly illegitimate. All exercise of church authority by ordained officers is viewed as a form of tyranny over the self-absorbed and self-empowered egalitarian church member. The trump card remains with the individual member, who can simply exercise his or her consumer choice by moving down the street to the next church. Ecclesiastical egalitarianism is promoting exactly the mind-set that our adversary longs for—prideful self-rule.

Visions of Order

The novelist and satirist Evelyn Waugh once commented that "we are all potential recruits for anarchy."[10] Waugh's point was that original sin renders every human inclined to destroying God's hierarchy and order and replacing it with our own barbarous self-rule. Satan does not need to create this desire within us. Instead, he merely needs to provide a spark to ignite our own latent sinful desires.

As Christians, we need to soberly assess our own propensity to embrace the worldview of the adversary by adopting a broad egalitarian mind-set. We need to recognize that the struggle we face in culture and the church is to maintain God's order in the face of the onslaught of Satan's chaotic initiatives. As Waugh noted, the struggle of the modern age is between "Christianity and Chaos."[11]

How do we resist adopting the worldview of our adversary? We begin by gaining a knowledge of God's Word, taking note of the hierarchies he has created, and then following through with respecting these in the family, workplace, public square, and church. Our resistance to egalitarianism must begin at the most fundamental level with the acceptance that God rules over

10. Evelyn Waugh, "Appendix: Conservative Manifesto," in *The Essays, Articles and Reviews of Evelyn Waugh*, ed. Donat Gallagher (Boston: Little Brown, 1984), 161–62.

11. Evelyn Waugh, "Converted to Rome," in *The Essays, Articles and Reviews of Evelyn Waugh*, 103.

us as the eternal King and has set in place a system of order that, while often occupied by imperfect leaders, nonetheless represents his divinely ordained will established to promote the effectiveness of his gospel and the glory of his Son.

The destructive effects of egalitarianism are neutralized every time we defer to those in authority above us. Egalitarianism is disarmed by simply following the pattern of Jesus Christ as described by the apostle Paul in his epistle to the Philippians:

> Do nothing out of selfish ambition or vain conceit, but in humility consider others better than yourselves. Each of you should look not only to your own interests, but also to the interests of others.
> Your attitude should be the same as that of Christ Jesus:
>
> Who, being in very nature God,
> > did not consider equality with God something to be
> > > grasped,
> but made himself nothing,
> > taking the very nature of a servant,
> > being made in human likeness.
> And being found in appearance as a man,
> > he humbled himself
> > and became obedient to death—
> > > even death on a cross!
> Therefore God exalted him to the highest place
> > and gave him the name that is above every name,
> that at the name of Jesus every knee should bow,
> > in heaven and on earth and under the earth,
> and every tongue confess that Jesus Christ is Lord,
> > to the glory of God the Father. (Phil. 2:3–11)

The Lord Jesus Christ, although being equal in essence with the Father, willingly submitted himself to the authority of the Father. This is the vision of order we need to adopt in our lives if we are to resist the worldview of our adversary.

5

Individualism

"Every Man Is an Island"

*Individualism kills individuality, precisely
because individualism has to be an "ism." ...
Men, instead of being themselves, set out to
find a self to be: a sort of abstract economic self
identified with self-interest. But while the self was
that of a man, the self-interest was generally that
of a class or a trade or even an empire. So far
from really remaining a separate self, the man
became part of a communal mass of selfishness.*[1]
—G. K. Chesterton

THE GREAT ENGLISH POET John Donne once wrote, "No man is an island entire of itself; every man is a piece of the continent, a part of the main."[2] The point Donne was making is that humanity is inherently interconnected. Donne argued that we simply cannot cut ourselves off from others and be

1. G.K. Chesterton, *Collected Works of G. K. Chesterton*, vol. 34 (Ignatius Press: San Francisco, 1990), 478.
2. John Donne, *Meditation XVII*.

truly human. We need each other. We need community. To be human means that we are connected to the community of humanity, not only those who are alive, but also those who have gone before us and those who will follow us. We are connected to our ancestors and to our progeny. We are, as Donne put it, "involved in mankind."

In our world today, however, this interconnectedness is being realized on only a superficial level. While politicians and multinational corporations give lip service to being "global citizens" and hundreds of millions are involved in Internet social networking communities, people are more self-absorbed than ever. In our world, every man is an island. Instead of being "involved in mankind," we are *involved* in ourselves. We all bow the knee to the idol of individualism.

In this chapter, we will explore how our modern love affair with individualism conflicts with a God-centered worldview. We will see that while the Bible does emphasize the inestimable value of each individual, it constantly calls us to subordinate our own self-interest to the needs of others. We will also see how our adversary is using our love affair with individualism to undermine God's authority, to destroy the tapestry of our world, and to divide the body of the church.

The Biblical Worldview: Life in Covenant Community

In America, and in much of the remainder of the West, individualism is celebrated as a social good. In our world, the individual is sovereign. But the biblical worldview is quite different, as D. A. Carson notes: "Although the Bible leaves ample scope for individuals, both precept and underlying assumptions make much more of corporate values than does our culture: the value of family and the importance of the covenant people of God as a body, are constantly reinforced."[3] The biblical worldview reminds us that we are in need of one another and

3. D. A. Carson, *The Gagging of God* (Grand Rapids: Zondervan, 1996), 47.

that life is best lived in the context of a covenant community. According to the biblical worldview, the corporate is more important than the individual. This principle is emphasized in many places in Scripture.

A Trinitarian Community

The first place we find this emphasis on life in covenant community is within the Trinity. The fact that God reveals himself as one God existing in three persons reveals that community is part of the nature of God. As Douglas Kelly puts it, "the true God has never existed as a single, solitary individual, 'cut-off' as it were, in lonely isolation within Himself."[4] The Trinity exists in a perpetually loving community, communion, and covenant. Reformed theologians have long noted that before creation there existed an intra-Trinitarian covenant in which the persons of the Trinity agreed to perform their respective roles to accomplish the redemption of the elect. This covenant is referred to as the *covenant of redemption*. The Trinity reveals that God is a relational God. As one theologian expressed it, "In himself he is a God of communion."[5]

Created for Community

Given that God reveals himself as a God who lives in Trinitarian community, it should not surprise us that the pinnacle of his creative work was created to mimic this relational inclination. Man was created for community. Adam was created as a social and relational being. First, he was created to personally relate to God through covenant, but he was also created to personally relate to other human beings through covenant. We see Adam's need for human companionship soon after his creation when God declared, "*It is not*

4. Douglas F. Kelly, *Systematic Theology*, vol. 1 (Fearn, Ross-shire, UK: Mentor, 2008), 274.

5. J. van Genderen & W. H. Velema, *Concise Reformed Dogmatics* (Phillipsburg, NJ: P&R Publishing, 2008), 160.

good for the man to be alone. I will make a helper suitable for him" (Gen. 2:18). God created a helper for Adam, and Adam entered into covenant marriage with Eve. Soon after this, Adam and Eve procreated according to God's command, and the community of the family was created. Eventually mankind's communal affiliations expanded to include tribes and nations. Man, as the image-bearer of the relational God, was created to live in community.

The Communion of the Saints

The biblical emphasis on the community over the individual reaches its pinnacle in the description of the church found in the New Testament. Here we learn the extraordinary truth that God's people are not a collection of isolated individuals, but rather they are the "people of God," "the body of Christ," the "temple of the Holy Spirit," and "the bride" of Christ. While modern Western Christianity emphasizes the individual experience, a "me and Jesus mentality," the New Testament emphasizes the corporate nature of Christian experience. When Paul speaks to the church, he most often employs the second-person plural *you*—he speaks to the church as community. Paul reminds us that as Christians we are called to serve one another and that all members of Christ's body are intimately interconnected:

> Just as each of us has one body with many members, and these members do not all have the same function, so in Christ we who are many form one body, and each member belongs to all the others. (Rom. 12:4–5)

Christians, as God's new creation in Christ Jesus, are created to live in covenant community with one another.

The Trinity, the creation of man, and the church all reveal a distinct pattern of placing the importance of community over the needs of the individual. God created mankind to live in covenant relationship with him and with each other. According to the worldview of the Bible, no man is an island.

The Worldview of the Adversary: The Self-Absorbed Life

Given the emphasis God places on living our lives in community where the needs of the individual are subordinated to the life of the community, it should not surprise us that our adversary seeks to promote exactly the opposite. Satan desires to create a world system in which mankind acts out of self-interest, totally disregarding the needs of others. Unbridled individualism is one of the most powerful weapons in the arsenal of our adversary. Satan wants us to embrace and live the self-absorbed life.

Unfortunately, Satan has been very effective in seducing mankind into embracing individualism as a way of life. Since the days of the Enlightenment, individualism has won the day in most Western cultures, and it is rapidly infecting the entire world. Cultures that once embraced the importance of family and community are buying in to the Western mantra of individualism. This unmitigated self-indulgence is destroying the fabric of our culture and the church, and ultimately, in a great irony, it also leads to the destruction of the self.

A Culture of Narcissism

Just at the turn of the new millennium, Harvard social scientist Robert D. Putnam published a book entitled *Bowling Alone: The Collapse and Revival of American Community.*[6] In this best-selling book, Putnam describes the social changes in America that have led to the collapse of community. He attributes blame for the demise of community in America to a variety of factors, including the pressures of time and money, mobility and suburban sprawl, technology and mass

6. New York: Simon and Schuster, 2000.

media, and the breakdown of the traditional family. But Putnam pins the greatest blame for the decline of community on a generational shift that occurred in America. He notes that the World War II generation was incredibly community-minded, being drawn together in solidarity around a common enemy, but succeeding generations have progressively detached themselves from community involvement of all forms. These post–World War II generations are, as Putnam puts it, "Bowling Alone."

The origins of our modern self-absorption can be traced back to philosophers such as Thomas Hobbes (1588–1679), John Locke (1632–1704), and Immanuel Kant (1724–1804). According to Russell Kirk, Hobbes viewed society as "a collection of selfish individuals, kept from one another's throat by the sword of the absolute monarch."[7] Kirk notes that Locke had "nothing to say about the Christian view of society as a bond between God and man," but that rather, Locke viewed society as composed of isolated individuals, a "kind of social atom."[8] The German philosopher Kant took this radical individualism to the level of transcendence. Kant viewed man as an autonomous agent who engaged the universe through pure reason. As Stanley Grenz notes, Kant "accorded little significance to any role played by human communities."[9]

The radical individualism promoted by Hobbes, Locke, and Kant did not simply remain thoughts in the heads of ancient philosophers; this idea became inculcated into our culture, laws, and mores. There is no place in the world where individualism has found more fruitful soil than in America. Rugged individualism is part and parcel of the American ethos. We are a John Wayne culture. At one point in our history, when Christianity was more dominant, this individualism promoted self-

7. Russell Kirk, *The Roots of American Order* (Washington, DC: Regnery Gateway, 1991), 271.

8. Ibid., 287.

9. Stanley J. Grenz, *A Primer on Postmodernism* (Grand Rapids: Eerdmans, 1996), 80.

sacrifice and heroism, but as the light of Christianity dimmed, our love affair with individualism morphed into something entirely selfish. D. A. Carson comments on this decline in the nature of individualism in American culture:

> In one context, individualism breeds courage, an entre-preneurial spirit, individual heroism, self-denial, deferred gratification, and thrift. It may accent values such as duty, honor, and industry. But if for whatever reasons the cultural values change, individualism can easily become a factor that reinforces narcissism, self-indulgence, instant gratification, self-promotion, and greed.[10]

When America's values declined in the post–World War II generation, our heroic individualism gave way to self-indulgence.

Our self-absorbed individualism has had profound effects on our culture. For example, consider how the view of marriage has changed in our culture. Marriage was once thought of as the union of two people into one for life, but now marriage is viewed as a flimsy contractual arrangement between two companions who agree to temporarily live together until their individual needs are no longer satisfied by the arrangement. Wendell Berry describes this modern individualistic view of marriage:

> Marriage, in what is evidently its most popular version, is now on the one hand an intimate "relationship" involving (ideally) two successful careerists in the same bed, and on the other hand a sort of private political system in which rights and interests must be constantly asserted and defended. Marriage, in other words, has now taken the form of divorce: a prolonged and impassioned negotiation as to how things shall be divided.[11]

10. Carson, *Gagging of God*, 47.
11. Wendell Berry, *What Are People For?* (New York: North Point Press, 1990), 180.

Instead of two becoming one in marriage, the modern version results in something more akin to a temporary collective bargaining agreement.

Our individualism has also led to a culture absorbed with acquiring material possessions. Personal consumption has replaced delayed gratification and thrift. The financial crisis of 2008 was caused by this spirit of radical individualism. The bubble in residential real estate was inflated by a series of individuals seeking to satisfy their own wants while neglecting to consider the broader societal impact of their avarice. Home buyers overextended themselves because they perceived that they deserved that house. Mortgage brokers slacked on their underwriting because they knew they could make a quick profit and pass the problem off to investment bankers. In turn, the investment bankers purchased subprime mortgages because they knew they could profit from repackaging them and selling them at great profit to greedy investors.

Nowhere along this chain of radical individualism did anyone pause to consider the potential damage that could be caused to others by their individual actions. The results for society have been devastating. As I write this book, America is experiencing one of its deepest recessions. Near double-digit unemployment, millions of foreclosed homes, and billions of dollars of government debt have resulted.

While Putnam accurately assesses and identifies the various social factors that have contributed to the rapid rise of individualism in American culture, he does not penetrate to the deeper spiritual issues that have led to the collapse of community. Self-love and self-absorption are ultimately products of sin. Whereas Jesus commands his children to love one another, our culture commands us to love ourselves. This self-love is rampant in our culture, and it is fraying the fabric of our society. It is resulting in the state's becoming the de facto community, replacing other historical social networks. In a great irony, our radical individualism is resulting in a reduction of personal liberty as we walk the road to serfdom. Our individualism has bred a culture of narcissism.

A Church of Narcissism

The spirit of radical individualism is also undermining the purpose and work of the church. Individualism compromises the authority of the church, the focus of the church, and the outreach of the church.

Undermining the Authority of the Church. The authority of the church is undermined by individualism because church members frequently view themselves as the final ecclesiastical authority on biblical interpretation and biblical discipline. This phenomenon is present in the megachurches of the broader evangelical world, but it is also manifesting itself in the Reformed churches. In his book *Recovering the Reformed Confession*, R. Scott Clark describes how the Reformed have become increasingly uneasy with their own confessional past. He notes that many in the Reformed church have adopted a "fundamentally individualistic approach to Scripture and tradition" that places their individual private judgments above the corporate and confessional voice of the church.[12] This move toward individual sovereignty in biblical interpretation is antithetical to the Reformed tradition.

The Reformation was not a monolithic development. Several strains of theology grew out of the Reformation. Most historians contend that there were three main divisions in the Reformation: the radical (or Anabaptist) movement, the Lutheran movement, and the Reformed movement. One of the things that separated the Reformed from the radical wing of the Reformation was its resistance to the private interpretation of Scripture that predominated in this movement. The Reformed rejected the idea that the biblical interpretations of

12. R. Scott Clark, *Recovering the Reformed Confession* (Phillipsburg, NJ: P&R Publishing, 2008), 27.

"prophetic" individuals and the theological layman were on par with the authority of the corporate creeds and confessions of the church. The Reformed rejected the idea of papal infallibility regarding the interpretation of Scripture, but they also rejected the idea of individual or private infallibility regarding the interpretation of Scripture.

This spirit of individualism most often manifests itself when a church member maintains an interpretation of Scripture that is contrary to the confession of his or her church. In most Reformed churches, members are not required to subscribe to the confession, but they normally do vow to submit to the teaching authority of the church and to not be divisive to the body. Yet many today disregard these vows. Whereas traditionally a church member who held an interpretation different from that of the church of which he was a member would keep these matters to himself, today it is common for members to attempt to force their private interpretations on others and openly rebel against the teaching of the church.

The spirit of individualism also manifests itself in the process of church discipline. In the face of correction from a church body, many choose to simply leave and find another church rather than submit to the correction of their elders. The bonds of membership and the vows undertaken are subordinated to the personal discretion and opinions of the church member. All a member has to do is take his Bible and move down the street to a new church.

These manifestations of individualism in the church undermine its work and ministry. But it is not just the laity that has given in to the spirit of individualism. Reformed elders and ministers seem very willing to place their own interpretations and beliefs above the corporate confessions of the church. The confessions too quickly become something to wield against others' aberrant teachings, yet many ministers have no qualms in exceeding the confessions' teachings when it comes to their own pet doctrines.

Undermining the Focus of the Church. The focus of the church is undermined by individualism because it has led church members into believing that the reason the church exists is to meet their individual needs and desires. The Bible calls us to make God and his mighty deeds the focus of the church, but because individualism has so pervaded our minds, most church members believe that the church is about them. In our individualistic culture, the church becomes just another service provider vying for the attention of self-indulgent consumers of religion.

Individualism has impacted many aspects of the church's ministry. One example of this impact can be seen in the music of the church. Much of contemporary worship music is riddled with first-person pronouns. We sing much more about ourselves than we do about God. Individualism has also influenced preaching. While preaching should be applied to the life of the individual, many modern sermons are *entirely* oriented to the individual. Many sermons are void of objective truth about God and instead are filled with subjective points meant to demonstrate personal relevance to the listener. In far too many sermons we learn much more about ourselves than we do about God.

Individualism is also impacting how the church functions. First, the spirit of individualism has required churches to add more and more services to attract and keep their members. Church members are no longer satisfied with Word, sacrament, and prayer; now they want a good youth group, Sunday school program, and small groups for every imaginable demographic. The proliferation of additional services requires additional staffing. At the same time, individualism is leading people to volunteer less often in their local congregations. Instead of coming to church to serve, people come to church to be served. D. A. Carson describes how this individualistic generation views the church: "The new generation does not readily think in terms of service to the church or to God, but in terms of what it can get out of it; they shop around for churches until they find a product they like."[13]

The spirit of individualism is undermining the focus of the church. The focus is no longer on God and personal service to the body of Christ. The focus is now on the service of the self. The communion of saints has given way to communion with the self.

Undermining the Outreach of the Church. Thus far we've seen how individualism is undermining the internal authority, discipline, focus, worship, and service of the church. But not only is individualism impacting the internal ministry of the church, it is also impacting its cultural outreach and ministry to the lost. Because of our cultural infatuation with individualism, religion is being jettisoned from the public square and sequestered in privatized life of the self. Our culture now views religion as a matter of individual preference rather than a subject of transcendent objective truth. The growth of privatized spirituality in our culture has delegitimized public proclamation and dialogue regarding the truth of the Bible and the claims of Christ on the lives of men and nations. In his book *Religion and Personal Autonomy*, Phillip Hammond contends that our overemphasis on the individual and on personal autonomy has led to a "third disestablishment" of religion.[14] In essence, individualism has resulted in a less effective public witness for the gospel by forcing religion into the category of a private and personal choice.

The Destruction of the Self

The great irony of our individualistic idolatry is that it is ultimately self-destructive. When we love and worship ourselves, we are doomed to destroy ourselves. It is only by deny-

---

13. Carson, *Gagging of God*, 50.

14. Phillip E. Hammond, *Religion and Personal Autonomy: The Third Disestablishment in America* (Columbia, SC: University of South Carolina Press, 1992).

ing ourselves that we truly find ourselves. This principle is at the heart of Jesus' teaching: "Whoever finds his life will lose it, and whoever loses his life for my sake will find it" (Matt. 10:39). Jesus reminds us that true life is found in the sacrificing of ourselves and our interests. It is only when we die to self that we can truly live for Christ. If Christians really lived this truth, the impact on our churches, and on our world, would be immeasurable. Given the power of losing ourselves for Christ, it should be no surprise that Satan has been operating an indefatigable advertising campaign to convince us of exactly the opposite viewpoint.

The Christian does not have to invent a new weapon to oppose the adversary when it comes to defeating this attack. The defense against the onslaught of individualism is to simply return to core principles of the Bible. We begin by remembering that everything is about God and his glory, not us and our needs. If we always keep God at the center of our lives and minds, we will never be overcome by self-absorption. Next we apply a self-sacrificing biblical approach to our families. According to the Bible, spouses are to help one another, parents are to sacrifice for their children, and children are to obey their parents. We then take this a step further by embracing the covenant community of the church. We begin by looking at the church as a place to serve God and others instead of a place that exists to serve us. We remain teachable and we respect our elders. We come to worship God and to receive his means of grace. We come to fellowship with others and to participate in the communion of the saints that transcends space and time. Finally, we take this spirit of selflessness out to a culture that is rapidly losing itself in a maelstrom of self-love. We minister mercy to the orphan, widow, and stranger within our gates. We proclaim the good news to those who are lost. We invite the self-absorbed to become absorbed into a communion of saints.

If we take up the gauntlet and begin living our lives according to God's Word, the scourge of unchecked individualism will simply evaporate from the landscape. What will be left is life as Christ would have us to live it: "Whoever finds his life will lose it, and whoever loses his life for my sake will find it" (Matt. 10:39). Lose *your* life and you will find it.

6

Materialism

All That Matters Is Matter

If any one age really attains by eugenics and scientific education the power to make its descendants what it pleases, all men who live after it are the patients of that power.
—C. S. Lewis, in "The Abolition of Man"[1]

THE TWENTIETH CENTURY produced two great novels that depicted equally horrifying, but differing, dystopias: George Orwell's *1984* (1949) and Aldous Huxley's *Brave New World* (1931). Orwell's dystopia was created by the heavy hand of the totalitarian state. In his vision of the future, Big Brother would be watching and controlling our every move and our every thought. Huxley's dystopia was of a different sort. His vision of the future pictured humanity as hedonistically indulging in psychological wonder drugs, the power of mass production (even in the area of human reproduction),

1. C.S. Lewis, *The Essential C.S. Lewis*, ed. Lyle W. Dorsett (New York: Touchstone, 1988), 450.

and technological innovation. Orwell predicted that the state would enslave us. Huxley, on the other hand, predicted that, in an effort to improve ourselves and our lives, we would enslave ourselves. From the vantage point of the first decade of the twenty-first century, it appears that Huxley was the more prescient of the two.

Our culture is currently preoccupied with self-improvement. Miracle drugs offer us not only the promise of physical well-being, but also the promise of sexual potency and the control of reproductive capabilities. Medical technology has given us not only heart transplants, but also Botox injections and breast implants. A panoply of drugs promise to remove anxiety, stress, and despair from our lives. Advances in computer technology hold out the promise that our failing organs can one day be replaced with computer chips. The merger of computer and biotechnologies holds out the promise that one day we may live forever by becoming "cyborgs," a mixture of man and machine. Biotechnology also offers the twin prospects of eternal life achieved through genetic cloning and the perfection of humanity by ridding our genetic code of imperfections.

While many of the advances in medical and computer technology have improved our lives in incalculable ways, they also raise immensely important ethical issues that threaten the very definition of what it means to be human. This is particularly true in areas where we are applying technology to help us transcend traditional notions of what it means to be human. Many are embracing the day when, through the promise of technology, humanity will enter a new state they refer to as *transhumanism*.[2] Transhumanism is built on the presupposition that there is nothing unique, special, or significant about human nature. According to the transhumanist, human nature is like supple clay that we can shape in any way

2. Transhumanism is also known as *posthumanism*.

that suits our needs, and technology has provided the tools to make this possible.

Ideas such as transhumanism raise the specter of Huxley's dystopian vision for humanity. But transhumanism and other belief systems like it are ultimately built on an underlying philosophical system called *materialism*. Dinesh D'Souza defines *materialism* as "the view that material things are the only reality and that knowledge of material objects is the only valid claim to knowledge; all else is simply a matter of belief or opinion."[3] Materialism denies the existence of a Creator and views man as a soulless machine.

In this chapter, we will explore how the worldview promoted by materialism runs contrary to a God-centered worldview. We will see that the Bible teaches us that there is something unique about human nature and that believing in a Creator is fundamentally necessary to understanding human nature. We will also see how our adversary uses ideas such as materialism not only to undermine a biblical worldview regarding human nature, but also to enslave us to ideologies and practices that are ultimately aimed at bringing about what C. S. Lewis referred to as "the abolition of man."

The Biblical Worldview: And God Made Man

In Psalm 100, the people of God sing a confession that encapsulates the biblical view of the relationship between God and humanity: "Know that the LORD is God. *It is he who made us, and we are his*; we are his people, the sheep of his pasture" (Ps. 100:3). This biblical view runs contrary to the predominant materialistic worldview operating in our culture. According to our culture, this psalm would read, "Know that we are god. It is chance that made us, and we are our own." When it comes to the origins, nature, and destiny of humanity, there could not be a more fundamental disagreement between the Bible

---

3. Dinesh D'Souza, *The Virtue of Prosperity* (New York: Touchstone, 2000), 225.

and our world. According to the Bible, we must grasp three fundamental principles in order to have a biblical worldview on human nature. We must understand that God made us, that he made us body and soul, and that, through our sin, we made ourselves imperfect.

God Made Us—We Are Not Our Own

The first thing we need to understand in order to maintain a biblical worldview regarding human nature is that we are creatures. Human nature is not something that emerged by chance and randomness. God voluntarily chose to create us: "Then God said, 'Let us make man in our image, in our likeness'" (Gen. 1:26). The Scripture is unequivocal about our origins: "So God created man in his own image" (Gen. 1:27). Human nature exists because God created us.

The implication of this reality is what the psalmist voiced in Psalm 100:3 when he declared that "we are his." Because humanity owes its existence to God, this means that God owns humanity. He is the Creator and we are the creature. Therefore, what we do with his property matters to him.

Human nature is not like an open-source computer program that we are licensed to fiddle with at our whim. God does call us to explore our biology and chemistry as a means of helping people and bringing glory to him, but he has not granted us liberty to manipulate human nature as we see fit. Because God is the Creator and landlord of our nature, we must always look to him for guidance and direction before we attempt to remodel his property. God made us; we are not our own.

God Made Us Body and Soul—We Are Not Mere Matter

The second component of a biblical worldview on human nature is the reality that God made humanity with a body *and* a soul. We are made of a material component (the body) and an immaterial component (the soul). Many theologians see a reference to these dual aspects of our nature in Genesis 2:7: "And the LORD God formed man from the dust of the ground and breathed into his nostrils the breath of life, and man became a living being." Herman Bavinck commented on this verse as follows:

> God is, first of all, demonstrable in the human soul. According to Genesis 2:7, man was formed from the dust of the earth by having the breath of life (*nismat hayyim*) breathed into his nostrils and so becoming a living soul (*nepes hayya, pysche zosa*). The breath of life is the principle of life; the living soul is the essence of man. By means of this combination Scripture accords to man a unique and independent place of his own and avoids both pantheism and materialism.[4]

Bavinck understood Genesis 2:7 as establishing the truth that man is more than mere matter—that instead, mankind is composed of both a physical body and an immaterial soul.

The Bible also teaches us that these two components of our being have differing values and different destinies. For example, Jesus is careful to remind us that the destiny of our souls is of greater significance than the current state of our physical bodies:

> Then Jesus said to his disciples, "If anyone would come after me, he must deny himself and take up his cross and follow me. For whoever wants to save his life will lose it, but whoever loses his life for me will find it. *What good will it be for a man if he gains the whole world, yet forfeits his soul? Or what can a man give in exchange for his soul?*" (Matt. 16:24–26)

Here Jesus clearly subordinates the needs of the physical body to the ultimate destiny of the soul. According to the Bible, the

4. Herman Bavinck, *Reformed Dogmatics*, vol. 2, ed. John Bolt, trans. John Vriend (Grand Rapids: Baker Academic, 2004), 555. There is some disagreement among Hebrew scholars about the exact translation of Genesis 2:7, particularly regarding the phrase rendered by the NIV "living being." Some translations render this "living soul."

body is valuable and should not be denigrated, but it is not as important as the immaterial aspect of human nature.

Our present earthly bodies are not as important as our souls because they have different destinies. The bodies that we possess in this world will not make the ultimate journey into the age to come, but our souls will. While each of us will have a body in the age to come, it will be a very different type of body from the one we have in this age. In fact, this present body must be destroyed for us to transition to the new body of the coming age. Paul makes this point in 1 Corinthians 15:

> So will it be with the resurrection of the dead. The body that is sown is perishable, it is raised imperishable; it is sown in dishonor, it is raised in glory; it is sown in weakness, it is raised in power; it is sown a natural body, it is raised a spiritual body. . . .
>
> I declare to you, brothers, that flesh and blood cannot inherit the kingdom of God, nor does the perishable inherit the imperishable. Listen, I tell you a mystery: We will not all sleep, but we will all be changed—in a flash, in the twinkling of an eye, at the last trumpet. For the trumpet will sound, the dead will be raised imperishable, and we will be changed. For the perishable must clothe itself with the imperishable, and the mortal with immortality. When the perishable has been clothed with the imperishable, and the mortal with immortality, then the saying that is written will come true: "Death has been swallowed up in victory." (1 Cor. 15:42–44, 50–54, quoting Isa. 25:8)

Our bodies are not destined to inherit the kingdom of God. We need new spiritual bodies to live in the age to come.

One implication of the truth that our material bodies are less significant than our immaterial souls is that we should be much more concerned with the welfare of the latter than the former. In other words, while we should care for our bodies as God's creation gift, our ultimate concern should be for the state of our souls. We should never allow the preservation and glorification of our bodies to become the preeminent focus of our lives.

A second implication of this truth is that we must never view human nature as composed of mere matter. We are not simply carbon-based life-forms. We are not mere machines. We are more than the mere firing of synapses and the functioning of organs. Human nature possesses an immaterial element that cannot be spliced, decoded, or examined under a microscope. God made us body and soul; we are not mere matter.

We Made Ourselves Imperfect—We Are Fundamentally Flawed

The final component of a biblical worldview on human nature is that we, through our sin, have made ourselves imperfect creatures and are thus unable to attain perfection in human nature in this age. When God created Adam, he made him perfect. Adam had a perfect body and a soul inclined toward holiness. Man was not made in corruption; like the rest of creation, he was made good. But because Adam willfully violated God's covenant, he brought imperfection to himself, to his progeny, and to the entire world. Adam's descendants have only added to this tsunami of imperfection by inheriting his sinful nature and by their own sins.

The condition of imperfection in which we find ourselves is, according to the Bible, an unalterable one, at least from a human perspective. The Bible teaches us that we are unable to change or perfect our nature. The Scriptures describe us as being dead in our sins and transgressions (Eph. 2:1). Humanity simply lacks the capacity to reach perfection in its own power. Only God can achieve that Herculean feat. God is the only hope for humanity and all creation, as Paul reminds us in Romans 8:

The creation waits in eager expectation for the sons of God to be revealed. For the creation was subjected to frustration, not by its own choice, but by the will of the one who subjected it, in hope that the creation itself will be liberated from its bondage to decay and brought into the glorious freedom of the children of God.

We know that the whole creation has been groaning as in the pains of childbirth right up to the present time. Not only so, but we ourselves, who have the firstfruits of the Spirit, groan inwardly as we wait eagerly for our adoption as sons, the redemption of our bodies. For in this hope we were saved. But hope that is seen is no hope at all. Who hopes for what he already has? But if we hope for what we do not yet have, we wait for it patiently. (Rom. 8:19–25)

The perfection of human nature cannot be achieved in this age and by human power. Instead, we must look to God for perfection, and we must wait for it patiently.

The implication of this biblical truth is that as Christians we should not subscribe to any system of thought advocating the idea that humanity can reach perfection outside of the redemptive work of Jesus Christ. It also reminds us that because we are imperfect, we are inclined to sin. This should make us less than sanguine about humanity's ability to morally manipulate scientific discoveries entirely for the social good. We should be suspect of those who exhibit great confidence in the idea that so-called advances in science will never be abused and perverted for selfish, and self-destructive, ends. We must never forget that we made ourselves imperfect; we are fundamentally flawed.

The biblical worldview of human nature is built on three foundational ideas: God made us, human nature consists of both body and soul, and we are imperfect creatures lacking the capacity to change that reality. It should come as no surprise that our enemy seeks to undermine each of these foundational ideas.

The Worldview of the Adversary: The Abolition of Man

Our enemy understands that at the center of the God-centered worldview is the idea that God is the Creator and we are his. The enemy knows that if he can convince us that God did not create us and has no power over us, then not only will we be inclined to forget about God and his Word, but we will also proceed down a path of self-destruction. The adversary desires nothing short of the absolute abolition of man.

In order to accomplish his goal, our enemy strives to convince us that we are made by chance, we are mere machines, and we can perfect ourselves. He attempts to convince us that we can change and transcend our very nature. He attempts to convince us to embrace materialism as our religion.

We Are Made by Chance

The first and most fundamental step in the strategy of the enemy is to convince us to buy in to the idea that we are made by mere chance. The most important first premise in the worldview of the adversary is that there is no Creator God. Our enemy wants us to believe that random natural forces can explain everything in the universe, including our existence.

Over the past several years, this materialistic and naturalistic view has received wide support through the writings of the so-called new atheists. Best-selling books such as Sam Harris's *The End of Faith*, Daniel Dennett's *Breaking the Spell*, Richard Dawkins' *The God Delusion*, Christopher Hitchens' *God Is Not Great*, and Victor Stenger's *The New Atheism* have all made the argument that humanity is the product of random natural forces. For example, Victor Stenger writes, "It is hard to conclude that the universe was created with a special, cosmic purpose for humanity."[5] Carl Sagan echoes Stenger's denial

5. Victor Stenger, *God: The Failed Hypothesis* (Amherst, NY: Prometheus Books, 2007), 161.

of a special role for humanity in the cosmos and calls us to rid ourselves of the "delusion that we have some privileged position in the universe."[6]

These scientists and pop-philosophers not only believe that we were made by chance, but also believe that the human race will be better off if it accepts this "truth." In the mind of many of the new atheists, much of the world's troubles can be traced to the belief in a Creator God and a special role for humanity in the creation. From the perspective of the new atheists, secular sins such as global warming and intolerance are by-products of believing that humanity was created by God.

It is interesting that the new atheists attribute sin to belief in a Creator because the Scripture expresses exactly the opposite relationship between sin and belief in a Creator. According to the Scriptures, sin is a consequence of *unbelief* in the Creator God. For example, consider how Paul connects sin directly to the denial of the Creator God in Romans 1:

> The wrath of God is being revealed from heaven against all the godlessness and wickedness of men who suppress the truth by their wickedness, since what may be known about God is plain to them, because God has made it plain to them. For since the creation of the world God's invisible qualities—his eternal power and divine nature—have been clearly seen, being understood from what has been made, so that men are without excuse.
>
> For although they knew God, they neither glorified him as God nor gave thanks to him, but their thinking became futile and their foolish hearts were darkened. Although they claimed to be wise, they became fools and exchanged the glory of the immortal God for images made to look like mortal man and birds and animals and reptiles.
>
> Therefore God gave them over in the sinful desires of their hearts to sexual impurity for the degrading of their

---

6. Carl Sagan, *Pale Blue Dot: A Vision of the Human Future in Space* (New York: Ballantine Books, 1994), 7.

bodies with one another. They exchanged the truth of God for a lie, and worshiped and served created things rather than the Creator—who is forever praised. Amen. (Rom. 1:18–25)

According to Paul, sin is a consequence of exchanging the truth of God for a lie and worshiping the created things rather than the Creator.

In his book *Understanding Paul*, Stephen Westerholm argues that Paul's view of the origin of sin is very similar to that espoused in the book of Proverbs. In Proverbs, according to Westerholm, sin is a product of living your life in disharmony with the created order.[7] The way we understand the created order, and thus live successfully, is by understanding the Creator of the order. Thus, Proverbs appropriately admonishes us that the "fear of the LORD is the beginning of knowledge" (Prov. 1:7). Westerholm summarizes the teachings of Proverbs and Paul regarding the relationship between sin and the denial of a Creator:

> If sin is inappropriate response to reality, the fundamental human sin (for Paul as for Proverbs) is the failure to respond appropriately to the Creator of all that is. Those who are in the presence of awesome natural or artistic beauty and yet fail to respond with wonder betray their own self-absorption and insensitivity. Similarly, for Paul, to enjoy life in a world created and ordered by divine goodness without responding with thanks to God is unnatural, perverse, sinful—and the root of all other sins. Other sins represent a refusal to live in harmony with some aspect of the divine order of creation. They follow inevitably from a refusal to give recognition to the Creator himself.[8]

True knowledge and righteous living flow from a humble acknowledgment and reverence of the One who made all

7. Stephen Westerholm, *Understanding Paul* (Grand Rapids: Baker Academic, 2004), 44–51.
8. Ibid., 48.

things. Sin, on the other hand, begins when one attempts to live his or her life without acknowledging the Creator. This is the sinner's equivalent of Proverbs 1:7: "Disregard of the Creator is the beginning of all unrighteousness."

The Scripture is clear in its warning that the denial of a Creator will result in a world filled with greater evil. This is why our adversary is so keen on promoting the dogma of the new atheists. If humanity accepts that we are made by chance, then sin can flourish in the fertile soil of our darkened minds and hearts.

We Are Mere Matter

The second prong of our enemy's strategy is to convince us that we are mere matter. Our adversary wants us to view humans as mere machines who are devoid of any immaterial and spiritual significance. This idea rests at the core of the philosophy of materialism. Dinesh D'Souza describes how materialism defines the nature of man: "From this perspective, man is a kind of intelligent robot, a carbon-based computer. Consequently, man should be understood in the same material terms in which we understand software programs."[9] Advocates of materialism, such as scientist and atheist Richard Dawkins, view human nature as something equivalent to software code. According to the view of materialism, we are nothing more than mere matter.

What is so dangerous about treating man as mere matter in our technological age? The danger is that once we embrace the idea that there is nothing unique about human nature and that we are simply machines, we can begin to treat human nature as just one more commodity. If we are mere matter, then it is easy to accept that a baby is merely a fetus. Once we accept that a baby is merely a fetus, then it is easy to argue that fetal tissue is a resource open to commercial and scientific exploitation.

9. Dinesh D'Souza, *What's So Great about Christianity?* (Carol Stream, IL: Tyndale House, 2007), 243.

Similarly, if we view humans as machines like computers, then don't we want the best operating systems possible? This type of thinking can lead to arguments about the use of selective abortions to rid humanity of genetic imperfections and potential birth defects. Aborting a child with Down syndrome becomes twisted into a heroic act of improving the human race and saving the child from a suboptimal life.

When human nature is reduced to mere matter, the doors are flung wide open to a variety of horrors that even Huxley could not have imagined—human cloning, genetic engineering, genetic discrimination, and fetal tissue harvesting. The Bible is unequivocal about the depraved nature of humanity. It tells us that our hearts cannot be trusted. It reminds us of our never-ending capacity to practice wickedness. History only serves to testify to these biblical realities. When we combine our technological capabilities with our depraved moral capacity, the prospects for humanity are grim. As Albert Einstein warned, "Technological progress is like an axe in the hands of a pathological criminal." The scary truth is that according to the Scriptures, we are all pathological spiritual criminals. The axe is in our untrustworthy hands.

If the enemy can convince us to view ourselves as mere matter, then the abolition of man will be an inevitable consequence. As C. S. Lewis warned, the future of humanity will be in the hands of "Conditioners," a close-knit group of scientific and philosophical oligarchs who will define what it means to be human. In his aptly titled book *The Abolition of Man*, Lewis penned the following warning to future generations:

> If any one age really attains by eugenics and scientific education the power to make its descendants what it pleases, all men who live after it are the patients of that power. Man's conquest of nature, if the dreams of some scientific planners are realized, means the rule of a few hundreds of men (in the present that is) over billions upon billions of men born later.

Human nature would be the last part of nature to surrender
to man, but then the battle would be won.[10]

Once a select segment of mankind assumes to itself the power
to define the parameters and meaning of human nature, then
this group will possess the perceived moral authority to do
whatever they want with it, and as Lewis put it, all men who
live after the assumption of this power will be "patients of
that power."

We Can Perfect Ourselves

The final prong in Satan's battle plan to undermine a biblical
understanding of human nature is to convince us that we can
perfect ourselves. Our enemy desires to persuade us to embrace
a utopian view regarding human nature. He longs to convince
us that we can achieve perfection without the help of God.

In the introduction to this chapter, I referred to a materialistic belief system known as *transhumanism*. One of the
core tenets of the transhumanist vision is that humanity will
continually improve itself and ultimately reach perfection.
The hope of the transhumanist is that through science and
technology we will render ourselves immortal. Through a
process of self-imposed natural selection, we will gradually
remove imperfections from the human condition and eventually evolve into a new and better being of existence.

While transhumanism is a modern phenomenon, the presuppositions that underlie its vision of human self-perfection
have roots extending back to the Enlightenment. C. Christopher Hook notes the close kinship between modern ideas such
as transhumanism and the Enlightenment, particularly with
regard to their conception of human nature:

While the names transhumanism and posthumanism have
been coined recently, the ideas they represent are anything

10. C. S. Lewis, *The Abolition of Man* (San Francisco: HarperSanFrancisco, 2001), 58.

but new. The underlying philosophical ideas are fully those of the Enlightenment, imbued with a healthy dose of postmodern ethical relativism. From the Enlightenment comes a fully reductionistic view of human life characteristic of that movement's materialistic empiricism; add to that a triumphalistic, technoutopian replacement of God with worship at the altar of scientism.[11]

Transhumanism represents a technological updating of the materialistic, empirical, and self-centered humanism of the Enlightenment philosophers.

The utopian vision of transhumanism is simply a new version of the age-old heresy of Pelagianism. Pelagius was a fourth-century British monk who denied the doctrine of original sin and championed the potential for human self-improvement through the operation of man's free will. Essentially, Pelagius believed that man could improve himself without the assistance of God's grace. In the end, transhumanism and thought systems like it are really offering the same lie. Transhumanism holds out the same lies that Satan uttered in the garden of Eden. It promises us that we can autonomously rule over creation, that we have no need for God, and that we will not surely die. This is why Satan desires us to embrace ideas such as transhumanism. Our enemy longs to have us believe that we can perfect ourselves without the intervention of the person, work, and grace of the Lord Jesus Christ.

The Future of the Human Race

The rapid advances of science and technology in the late twentieth and early twenty-first centuries pose great challenges to Christians. Science and technology have so greatly benefited humanity that many have become convinced to

---

11. C. Christopher Hook, "Techno Sapiens," in *Human Dignity in the Biotech Century*, ed. Charles W. Colson & Nigel M. de S. Cameron (Downers Grove, IL: InterVarsity Press, 2004), 85.

blindly embrace whatever they have to offer us. Science appears to offer us something that God cannot: a worldview that is built on concrete and empirical truths that require no faith. That worldview is known as *materialism*, and it seems to offer the promise of explaining everything. According to this worldview, man is merely a machine who was created by the forces of chance. His body is devoid of the immaterial, and he has no special significance in the universe. He lives in a world that, like him, is merely a machine also created by the forces of chance. Man is beholden to no one outside himself and has the innate potential to achieve his own perfection.

But upon deeper reflection, we realize that the supposedly objective and concrete worldview of materialism is really a facade. In the end, materialism is just another belief system. As D'Souza notes, "Naturalism and materialism are not scientific conclusions; rather, they are scientific premises. They are not discovered in nature but imposed upon nature. In short they are articles of faith."[12]

But the problem with the belief system of materialism is that the faith required to embrace this mechanistic worldview is simply unreasonable. Herman Bavinck, writing in the early part of the twentieth century, commented on the faith required to embrace a materialistic worldview:

> [The claim] "the world is a machine" sounds simple, but it demands too much of our faith that this brief formula should contain the answer to all that moves and lives, and that all thinking and striving, struggling and suffering on the part of man and humanity could be reduced, in the end, to a mechanical movement and would be the result of the pressure and thrust of soulless atoms. The world is never something that is self-evident.[13]

12. D'Souza, *What's So Great about Christianity?*, 165.
13. Herman Bavinck, *Essays on Religion, Science, and Society*, ed. John Bolt, trans. Harry Boonsra and Gerrit Sheeres (Grand Rapids: Baker Academic, 2008), 110.

Humanity is more than a conglomeration of "soulless atoms," and the world around us is not "self-evident." If we are to really understand our world, and ourselves, we need to acknowledge that we are not our own, that we are not mere matter, and that we are fundamentally flawed.

The Christian is called to take every thought captive to Christ and to tear down the strongholds of our enemy. This means that we must combat such ideas as materialism, naturalism, and transhumanism. We must fight a counterinsurgency against any belief system that eliminates the reality of the Creator and reduces humanity to a soulless machine. Nigel M. de S. Cameron calls on all Christians to "resist the commodification of humankind."[14]

How do we accomplish this? We accomplish it by never ceding the reality that there is a Creator, by defending the fact that humanity is more than mere matter, and by persistently proclaiming humanity's desperate need of a Savior. We accomplish it by becoming active participants in the academic and political debates of our time. The battle for biblically defined human dignity will have to be fought in the halls of the university and the halls of Congress.

But this battle must not only be fought in the university and the public square; it must also be fought in the intimacy of our lives. Christians can testify to the reality of a benevolent Creator and the uniqueness of humanity by simply living their lives in faithful adherence to the order of our Creator. In other words, we can defeat the worldview of our adversary by seemingly mundane, yet powerful things, such as raising our children in the nurture and admonition of the Lord. As Wendell Berry put it, "We have no need to contrive and dabble at 'the future of the human race'; we have the same pressing need that we have always had—to love, care for, and teach our

14. Nigel M. de S. Cameron, "Christian Vision for the Biotech Century," in *Human Dignity in the Biotech Century*, 39.

children."[15] When we live our lives according to God's design, we testify not only to his existence, but to the fact that we are more than random, soulless machines.

Finally, we must fight this battle in the pulpits of our land. We must continually proclaim the reality that humanity's longing for immortality and perfection cannot be achieved in a test tube or through the manipulation of our genetic code. We must tell people that these longings can be achieved only through the redemptive work of Jesus Christ.

15. Wendell Berry, *What Are People For?* (New York: North Point Press, 1990), 188.

7

Consumerism

"Shop Till You Drop"

What we revere is what we resemble,
either for ruin or restoration.
—G. K. Beale[1]

THE OTHER DAY I received an advertisement in the mail from a new church in my area. The advertisement began with a question, "Fun at church?" and the following insightful answer was provided: "Yup." The advertisement listed what the church could offer me: "free coffee," "free rockin' music," and "free fun for kids." The church described its goal as "church done differently" and listed the following adjectives to describe its worship and fellowship: "casual," "modern," "biblical" (apparently this ranks third in importance!), "friendly," and "meaningful." The advertisement also included photographs of young, attractive, white, suburban-looking

1. G.K. Beale, *We Become What We Worship: A Biblical Theology of Idolatry* (Downers Grove, IL: Intervarsity, 2008), 16.

people smiling from ear to ear. Needless to say, I chose not to attend the opening service of this church.

While this advertisement did not persuade me to attend the new church, it did reveal to me the extent to which consumerism has infiltrated the mind-set of the church. The presuppositions giving rise to this "marketing technique" reveal that this church has a specific demographic in mind and is trying to provide that demographic with what it wants. The young, white, affluent families of suburbia are interested in coffee, rockin' music, and fun for their kids. These consumers of religion want to make sure that the church will serve them, and the church is more than happy to oblige.

One of the ideas undermining our minds, both in the culture and in the church, is the idea of consumerism. Residing at the core of the ideology of consumerism is the belief that personal happiness is advanced through the acquisition, consumption, and enjoyment of material possessions. Nowhere in the world has this ideology caught on with more vigor than in the United States. In America, consumer spending makes up 70 percent of our economy. That is a staggering number. Americans pursue their happiness by acquiring stuff, and every purveyor of goods and services, including the church, caters to the taste of the insatiable American consumer. But this ideology ultimately does not deliver on its promises. Instead of bringing us happiness, it brings emptiness. Even more troubling, the *ideology* of consumerism ultimately beckons us to engage in the *idolatry* of consumerism.

In this chapter, we will explore how the principles of consumerism conflict with a God-centered worldview. We will see that the Bible has much to say about how Christians should view wealth and possessions. We'll also see how our adversary is using the idea of consumerism to eviscerate meaning from our culture and encourage idolatry in our churches.

The Biblical Worldview: Christ Our Inheritance

Historically, Christians have held a variety of opinions regarding what constitutes a Christian worldview of material wealth and possessions. On one end of the spectrum are those Christians who become convinced that the only proper response to material possessions is to renounce them entirely. Some Christians believe that one can live for God only through a vow of poverty or an ascetic lifestyle. On the other end of the spectrum are those promoters of the "prosperity gospel," who claim that God wants us all to be wealthy and that material possessions are always a sign of God's blessing. When it comes to the topic of wealth, Christians have vastly different views, but which view is right? The best way to develop a biblical worldview about maintaining a proper relationship to material possessions is by looking at a few core principles taught by the Scriptures.

It's Okay to Own Things: The Eighth Commandment

The first principle that emerges from a survey of the Bible regarding material possessions is that it is proper for believers to own things. The Bible supports and defends the idea of private property. This principle is implicitly taught in the eighth commandment: "You shall not steal" (Ex. 20:15). Philip Ryken notes how the eighth commandment supports the idea of private property: "By saying 'You shall not steal,' God indicated that people have a right to own their private property. Otherwise, the whole concept of stealing would fail to make any sense."[2] God defends the right of private property with the full force of his holy law.

But the Bible does not simply defend the right to private property; it also supports the idea of the legitimate and honest accumulation of wealth. For instance, consider the wisdom of Proverbs 10:4: "Lazy hands make a man poor, but diligent

2. Philip Graham Ryken, *Written in Stone* (Wheaton, IL: Crossway, 2003), 174.

hands bring wealth." Another proverb tells us of the goodness of leaving a material inheritance to our children: "A good man leaves an inheritance for his children's children, but a sinner's wealth is stored up for the righteous" (Prov. 13:22). The Bible tells us that it is an appropriate goal to acquire wealth through hard work.

In addition to God's law and wisdom, the Bible also provides us with anecdotal evidence of God's approval of the acquisition and possession of material wealth. Think of how God enriched Old Testament saints such as Abraham, David, and Solomon. Consider how God used wealthy New Testament saints such as Phoebe, Lydia, and Aquila and Priscilla to support and advance the work of his kingdom.

Through law, wisdom, and example, the Bible teaches us that wealth and material possessions represent legitimate blessings to the believer. But like so many other blessings, wealth can be misused in a way that renders it biblically illegitimate.

It's Not Okay to Worship Things: The First Commandment

While the Bible does not treat wealth and material possessions as inherently evil, it does sternly warn us that the *love* of money is the "root of all kinds of evil" (1 Tim. 6:10). The blessing of wealth turns into wickedness when wealth assumes a place in our life that is to be occupied only by God. We run into problems when we worship our wealth.

Once again we are guided here by God's holy law. The first commandment states, "You shall have no other gods before me" (Ex. 20:3). Wealth and material possessions can become a false god when we begin to revere them. But how do we know whether we are violating this commandment and falling into this sin of idolatry?

Philip Ryken helps us to analyze this issue in our hearts by suggesting that we take a two-pronged test. First, Ryken says that we should ask ourselves what we love: "When your mind is free to roam, what do you think about? How do you spend your money? What do you get excited about? A false god can be any good thing that we focus on to the exclusion of God. It could be a sport or recreation. It could be a hobby or personal interest. It could be an appetite for the finer things in life. It could be career ambition."[3] Ryken then calls us to ask ourselves about where we are placing our trust. Ryken challenges us to think about where we turn in times of trouble because this reveals where our hearts are. He notes that in times of trouble, people tend to trust in things such as their addictions, sex, shopping, or other obsessions. Here Ryken quotes Martin Luther, who said, "Whatever thy heart clings to and relies upon, that is properly thy God."[4] Jesus made this point even more poignantly in his Sermon on the Mount: "For where your treasure is, there your heart will be also" (Matt. 6:21).

While owning things is biblically legitimate, having these things own us and our affections is not. The Bible teaches us that we are not to covet other people's possessions (Ex. 20:17) and that greed is ultimately a form of idolatry (Col. 3:5). To put it succinctly, the Bible commands us not to love or trust in anything except the Lord our God. He alone is worthy of our worship and holy reverence. According to the biblical worldview, it's okay to own things, but it is not okay for us to worship things.

Other Principles of Heavenly Economics

So far we've seen that the general principle taught by Scripture is that the accumulation of material wealth and possessions is legitimate as long as we don't fall into idolatry. Thankfully, the Bible provides us with guidance on how to avoid engaging in idolatry in this sphere of our life. The Bible provides us with several other important principles of heavenly economics.

3. Ibid., 66.
4. Ibid.

One of these principles is that we must always remember the temporal limitations of wealth and possessions. The Bible teaches us that the significance of the things we own in this life is limited to this life. For example, James tells us in his epistle that a rich man will "pass away like a wild flower" (James 1:10). Psalm 49 also emphasizes the temporal nature of wealth:

> Do not be overawed when a man grows rich,
>   when the splendor of his house increases;
> for he will take nothing with him when he dies,
>   his splendor will not descend with him. (Ps. 49:16–17)

Proverbs expresses this principle in these words: "Wealth is worthless in the day of wrath, but righteousness delivers from death" (Prov. 11:4). Of course, Jesus also teaches the principle in the Sermon on the Mount:

> Do not store up for yourselves treasures on earth, where moth and rust destroy, and where thieves break in and steal. But store up for yourselves treasures in heaven, where moth and rust do not destroy, and where thieves do not break in and steal. (Matt. 6:19–20)

Another principle of heavenly economics is that we can acquire intangible things in this life that are worth much more than any form of material possession. For example, consider the following teaching from the sage of Proverbs: "How much better to get wisdom than gold, to choose understanding rather than silver!" (Prov. 16:16). Wisdom and understanding are more valuable than gold. Similarly, Proverbs teaches us that acquiring faithfulness in our walk with God is more valuable than earthly riches: "Better a poor man whose walk is blameless than a rich man whose ways are perverse" (Prov. 28:6). This principle helps us to properly appraise and prioritize the acquisition of wealth in our lives.

A final principle of heavenly economics is that our riches are ultimately found in our relationship with Jesus Christ. The apostle Paul calls us to count everything else in our life as rubbish in comparison to the surpassing greatness of knowing Jesus Christ (Phil. 3:8). Paul also reminds us that our spiritual, incorruptible, and enduring heavenly inheritance is acquired only by our being coheirs with Jesus Christ (Rom. 8:17).

The biblical worldview of wealth and possessions is quite simple. The Bible teaches us that legitimately acquired wealth is to be enjoyed as a blessing from God. But the Bible warns us to never allocate our affections to our possessions and to never place our trust in them. The Bible reminds us continually about the temporal nature of wealth and its subordination to other intangible things of value, such as wisdom, understanding, and faithfulness. Finally, the Bible reminds us that our riches are in Christ Jesus. The biblical worldview of wealth can be distilled to this one principle: it's proper for us to own things, but it is *not* proper for these things to own us. The Bible calls us to worship God and not our stuff.

The Worldview of the Adversary: Worship Your Stuff

While the biblical worldview calls us to keep our possessions in proper perspective, our adversary seeks to convince us to do exactly the opposite. Satan's goal is to encourage us to find our meaning and satisfaction in material things. He wants us to be primarily consumers of things, rather than worshipers of God. His aim is to get us to worship our stuff.

When one surveys modern Western culture, particularly in America, it appears that the adversary has been waging a very successful campaign. Seventy percent of the American economy is made up of consumer spending. Americans are the consummate consumers. America's national avarice for stuff is wreaking havoc on our national pocketbook and on our spirituality. The consumerism of our age is turning us away from

God. As D. A. Carson put it, "The endemic consumerism of the age feeds our greed, and even defines our humanity: we are not primarily worshipers, or thinkers, or God's image-bearers, or lovers, but consumers."[5] We are worshiping our stuff.

As worshipers of material possessions, we have even constructed temples worthy of our avarice. Every major metropolitan area in America has one or more of these temples where the devoted can worship the pursuit of possessions. This temple is, of course, the mall. Gene Veith notes, "The mall stands as a temple to consumerism and all of its values—comfort, affluence, convenience, and fashion. The Middle Ages had its cathedrals; the modern age had its factories; the postmodern age has its shopping malls."[6]

By promoting consumerism, Satan is enabling us to violate the first commandment. He is encouraging us to worship a false god. This false worship is affecting both our culture and the church.

Consumerism and Our Culture

The impact that unbridled consumerism is having on our culture is difficult to overstate. Some of the negative impact of consumerism is easily quantifiable. The great financial crisis that emerged in the fall of 2008 and that continues to ripple through the economy as I am writing this book was fueled in many ways by America's insatiable appetite for things. People purchased houses they couldn't afford. People used their houses as ATMs to purchase other stuff, such as new cars and big-screen televisions. Consumer debt skyrocketed to unprecedented levels. Eventually, the house of cards came crashing down, and the overleveraged paid for their avarice.

But the negative effect of consumerism on our culture is not limited to dollars and cents. Consumerism ultimately taps our souls much more than it does our bank accounts. Unfet-

5. D. A. Carson, *The Gagging of God* (Grand Rapids: Zondervan, 1996), 463.
6. Gene Edward Veith Jr., *Postmodern Times* (Wheaton, IL: Crossway, 1994), 117.

tered consumerism leads our culture away from God. It does this in two ways.

Filling Us with Emptiness

The first way that consumerism is leading our culture away from God is by encouraging us to fill our lives with emptiness. Augustine once said that we are all made with a "God-shaped void." Only God can fill that void in us, but consumerism offers the false promise that stuff can fill our void. In this way, material possessions are offered to us by our culture as false gods claiming to satisfy our inner longings. Yet the false gods offered by consumerism, while temporarily satisfying us, ultimately leave us feeling empty. This emptiness often leads to despair and meaninglessness.

Tellingly, the Bible links idolatry to the concepts of vanity and emptiness. For instance, many of the Hebrew words used for idols in the Old Testament can be translated as "vanity" or "emptiness." Idolatry leads to emptiness. G. K. Beale also notes that the Old Testament uses another word for *idol* that can be translated as "thing of horror" or "thing of shuddering." Based on the meaning of this word, Beale concludes the following regarding the damaging impact of worshiping vain idols: "To worship such idols will bring only horror and dismay, not the peaceful bliss that is hoped for. But when we begin to resemble the idols of the world and spiritual harm is set in motion, we often don't feel the harm at first. Often we don't sense it until it is too late."[7] By worshiping the idols of consumerism, our culture is eviscerating its own soul. What is left is emptiness and disillusionment. As Dinesh D'Souza has noted, "many people discover that material possessions, however abundant and engaging, do not satisfy their deepest longings."[8]

7. G. K. Beale, *We Become What We Worship* (Downers Grove, IL: IVP Academic, 2008), 308.
8. Dinesh D'Souza, *The Virtue of Prosperity* (New York: Touchstone, 2000), 243.

Distracting Us

Consumerism not only leaves people feeling the horror of emptiness, but also serves as a great distraction. D'Souza contends that those obsessed with the pursuit of material possessions are not likely to think about their greater needs: "Such a person is so obsessed with improving his lifestyle that you cannot convince him that there is more to life than that."[9] Pursuing material possessions and wealth is for many people their entire life's work. They work eighty-hour weeks, neglecting family and faith, to keep the things they have and to acquire more.

Our culture, with its endless advertising and spacious malls, continually feeds new products and new distractions to us. In this sense, we live in unprecedented times. Os Guinness writes of the unparalleled consumer distractions of our age: "No civilization in history has offered more gifts and therefore has amplified the temptation of living 'by bread alone' with such power and variety and to such effect. In today's convenient, climate-controlled spiritual world created by the managerial and therapeutic revolutions, nothing is easier than living apart from God."[10] We have so many "things" to occupy our time, we never give thought to the great issues of life. Consumerism leaves our culture spiritually empty and mentally distracted.

Consumerism and the Church

Unfortunately, the devastating power of consumerism has also severely affected the church. This impact can be seen even in the architecture of our modern churches. Many new church buildings look remarkably similar to the temple of consumerism—the mall. Gene Veith writes, "Sometimes today churches resemble malls or theme parks, not only in their architecture, but in the way people think about them. Megachurches sometimes

9. Ibid.
10. Os Guinness, *Dining with the Devil* (Grand Rapids: Baker, 1993), 37.

resemble malls—with the parking lots, atriums, information booths, and shops featuring Christian merchandise."[11]

But the architectural influence of consumerism is not the biggest challenge faced by the church from the infiltration of consumerism. Consumerism is influencing the impact and theology of the church.

Consumerism and the Life of the Church: The Haggai Problem

Consumerism impacts the effectiveness of the church because it impacts the priorities of Christians when it comes to the use of their resources. In other words, the acquisition idolatry that permeates our wider culture has infected the church. The end result is that the church has to compete with the consumer desires of its members for the resources necessary to expand its influence in the local community. When it comes to our financial priorities, the church is dropping farther down the list as it competes with the cultural avarice to acquire consumer goods. The church is suffering from what I refer to as the "Haggai Problem."

Although ancient Israel did not have iPods, Amazon.com, or massive shopping malls, it still confronted the problem of consumerism. This should not be surprising, because consumerism is nothing but a new form of self-love and idolatry. We can witness Israel's struggle with this problem in the book of Haggai.

Haggai tells us of Israel's efforts to rebuild the temple of God, which had been destroyed by the Babylonians. The main obstacle to the completion of this work was a lack of resources. The people eventually concluded that this lack of resources was an indication that the time had not yet come to build the Lord's house. But God had a different interpretation of the situation. God, through his prophet Haggai, rebuked the Israelites for their misplaced financial priorities:

11. Veith, *Postmodern Times*, 118.

This is what the LORD Almighty says: "These people say, 'The time has not yet come for the LORD's house to be built.'"

Then the word of the LORD came through the prophet Haggai: *"Is it a time for you yourselves to be living in your paneled houses, while this house remains a ruin?"* (Hag. 1:2–4)

Haggai tells the people of Israel that the problem is not a lack of resources, but rather a competition for resources. The church was competing with the consumer desires of the people, and the church was losing. The people had "paneled houses," while God's house remained in ruins. This is the Haggai Problem, and it remains with us today.

Just as in Haggai's day, the church is hobbled in its efforts by having to compete for resources with people who prefer their modern equivalent of "paneled houses." How many church buildings suffer from disrepair in our age while our homes are filled with every modern amenity? How many pastors are underpaid and treated in ways we would never tolerate in our own workplaces? Our adversary is very happy to see us undermining the work of the church in this manner. The enemy seeks to subversively weaken the power of the church, and all he has to do is to convince us to make ourselves the priority. Unfortunately, convincing us to place our consumer desires above the needs of the church is an incredibly easy task, and the enemy has the entire culture to help cheer us on in this idolatry.

So how do we combat the Haggai Problem? We begin by examining our consumption habits and our financial priorities. We combat the problem of consumerism by following Haggai's advice to the people of Israel. Four times in his prophecy Haggai admonishes Israel with the following words: "Give careful thought to your ways" (1:5; 1:7; 2:15; 2:18). Haggai was calling the people to examine the priorities of their lives. We need to do the same today. We need to give careful thought to our ways and to resist the worldview of the adversary.

Consumerism and the Theology of the Church: The Problem of the Prosperity Gospel

Unfortunately, the Haggai Problem is not the only ill effect that consumerism is having on the life of the church. Consumerism impacts the church not only financially, but also theologically. Consumerism has led to the spawning of a new type of false gospel. This false gospel has been forged to fit the shape of the modern consumer mind and satisfy its cravings for financial prosperity. This iteration of the false gospel is often referred to as the *prosperity gospel*.

In his book *The Gagging of God*, D. A. Carson notes that among the various types of modern evangelicals is the one who is driven to wed his faith to his consumer idolatry. Carson describes this type of evangelical as one "who formally espouses the historic faith but whose heartbeat is for more and more of this world's goods, whose dreams are not for heaven and for the glory of God, but for success, financial independence, a bigger house, a finer car."[12]

Carson argues that this syncretism between consumerism and Christianity has permeated the Christian mind and alters how we understand God and evaluate our faith. According to Carson, the consumer mentality of our age becomes the ruler by which we measure all things in the church:

> The truth of the matter is that the consumer mentality authorizes people to judge all matters religious and theological by the simple criterion of whether or not they have been 'helped'—and the only people equipped to assess whether or not they have truly been helped are the people who claim to have been helped. Questions of truth, long-range effects, and purpose are all shunted aside.[13]

Once consumer criteria begin to serve as our yardstick for theological matters, we end up with a religion that attracts

12. Carson, *Gagging of God*, 465.
13. Ibid., 467.

marketers as pastors, church buildings that look like malls, and preaching that is oriented more to self-help than to salvation.

Consumerism has profoundly affected the evangelical mind and has brought an entirely new meaning to the term *church-shopping*. Biblical truth has been relegated to the level of just another consumer product that must constantly be "new and improved" to meet the demands of fickle religious consumers. Our adversary rejoices every time the church and its theology are shaped by the priorities of the world.

Our calling as Christians is to actively resist the onslaught of consumerism and the detrimental impact of the prosperity gospel. We carry out this calling by employing only one gauge for truth—the Bible. We must resist importing the criterion of consumerism into the church. The church is called to preach, teach, administer the sacraments, make and discipline disciples, and, most of all, glorify God in all that it does. The church is not called to meet the felt needs of every imaginable demographic group or to offer you a hot cappuccino and a scone on Sunday morning. Ultimately, we can resist consumerism in the church by reminding ourselves that the church does not exist to serve us, but rather that we exist to serve her. If we were to adopt such a mind-set, we would begin to see the true prosperity promised in the gospel.

Living the Good Life

Sometimes attacks on wealth and prosperity from a Christian perspective go too far. I don't want to make that mistake in this chapter. I believe that having and enjoying material things is *not* inconsistent with faithful Christian living. Perhaps I am naive, but like Dinesh D'Souza I believe a Christian can live "the good life and the life that is good."[14] The way we achieve this balance is by recalling and embracing the principles of a biblical worldview of wealth. We remember that enjoying

14. D'Souza, *The Virtue of Prosperity*, 254.

things is different from worshiping them. We remember the principles of heavenly economics, which always force us to use an eschatological metric to value the things in our lives. If we do this, we will keep the things that will pass away separate from the things that will endure.

While consumerism plagues our culture, we must also remember that, like all other forms of idolatry, it provides us with a point of contact to minister to people in need. As we've seen in this chapter, consumerism doesn't deliver on the promise to provide meaning and instead leaves people with a great void. While consumerism reigns, there is a growing sense among people in the modern world that there must be something more to life than gadgets and trinkets. For example, D'Souza writes, "Today more and more people are fully cognizant of the limits of materialism. They are searching for a sense of meaning, purpose, or something higher to which they can devote themselves."[15] This growing sense of disappointment with materialism opens a door for the gospel. We should grasp this opportunity to point people to the incomparable and enduring riches found in Christ Jesus. Nothing will undermine the work of our adversary more completely than calling people to embrace an inheritance that "can never perish, spoil or fade" (1 Peter 1:4).

15. Ibid., 244.

8

Relativism

"What Is Truth?"

Everything is relative in this world,
where change alone endures.[1]
—Leon Trotsky

AS I AM WRITING THIS BOOK, HSBC, a major interna-
tional banking institution, is running a television advertising campaign that displays a variety of people standing on a
"soapbox" and giving their views of various issues. One such
ad addresses the topic of the value of having children. In this
ad one woman declares, "I didn't want to be a mom. It took me
three months to love him. Now I can't imagine my life without
him." In the same ad a man declares, "Look around you—there's
a million, billion children. They don't need me to reproduce."
The advertising campaign is an attempt to celebrate diversity
and to convey the idea that the validity of values and morals
is something to be determined by every individual.

---

1. Leon Trotsky and Max Eastman, *The Revolution Betrayed* (Mineola, NY: Dover
Publications, 2004), 79.

What HSBC is celebrating is an idea known as *moral relativism*. Moral relativism maintains that there are no universal truths. Instead, truth is conditioned by an individual's circumstances, conditioning, and personal beliefs. D. A. Carson defines *moral relativism* as "the theory that denies absolutism and insists that morality and religion are relative to the people who embrace them."[2] Moral relativism takes truth out of the objective realm and places it firmly in the subjective realm of the individual. In terms of the HSBC commercial, morality is determined by each person as he or she stands on the soapbox.

In this chapter, we will explore how the idea of moral relativism serves to undermine a God-centered worldview. We will see that the Bible teaches us that morality and truth are objective ideas and are defined by God, not individual choice. We'll also see how our adversary is using the idea of moral relativism to fray the fabric of our culture and to confuse the doctrine and life of the church.

The Biblical Worldview: God's Unchanging Standard

When it comes to the topic of morality, the Bible speaks with an unequivocal and unwavering voice. In sharp contrast to our morally relativistic culture, the Bible teaches us that God has set forth and maintained an unchanging standard of right and wrong. This moral standard is like a thread woven throughout the entire tapestry of Scripture, from Genesis to Revelation. Theologians refer to God's unchanging moral standard as the *moral law*.

God's moral law serves as the guidance system for all Christian ethics. The moral law is the biblical worldview. Therefore, we must understand the nature of God's moral law so that we may live our lives in accord with it and resist adopting the moral relativism that is so prevalent in our surrounding culture.

2. D. A. Carson, *Becoming Conversant with the Emerging Church* (Grand Rapids: Zondervan, 2005), 31.

The Moral Law Is a Reflection of God's Holiness

The Bible teaches us that the moral standards set forth by God reflect his holy character. In other words, God's moral law is a lens through which we can better understand what he is like. Just as the laws that are adopted by a particular society or political party reveal something about the nature and priorities of that society or political party, so, too, the laws of God reveal something about his nature. The moral law is inextricably linked to God. It is a manifestation of his holiness. This is why our adversary seeks to distort and dismember God's moral law. Satan knows that those who dismiss the moral law will also dismiss the Giver of that law.

The Moral Law Is a Universal Standard

The Bible also reveals that the moral law of God universally applies. The moral law is not something just for believers; instead, it is meant to serve as the moral compass for every human being. Long before God wrote his moral law on tablets of stone and gave them to Moses, he wrote these same laws on the heart of Adam. Humans were created as God's image-bearers, and thus God implanted within the human heart the knowledge of his holy law, which reflects his image. All human beings carry this universal standard in their hearts, and God judges all human behavior by this measure. The apostle Paul writes of this reality in his epistle to the Romans, in which he declares that the Gentiles have the "requirements of the law . . . written on their hearts" (Rom. 2:15). The biblical worldview maintains the idea that moral standards are not culturally contextualized, but rather are universal principles applying to all mankind.

The Moral Law Is Immutable

During his great Sermon on the Mount, Jesus declared the following regarding the moral law:

> Do not think that I have come to abolish the Law or the
> Prophets; I have not come to abolish them but to fulfill them.
> I tell you the truth, until heaven and earth disappear, not the
> smallest letter, not the least stroke of a pen, will by any means
> disappear from the Law until everything is accomplished.
> (Matt. 5:17–18)

Here Jesus teaches that God's law is not subject to change. God gives us one standard that applies in all ages. The moral law etched by God's finger is indeed written in stone; it was designed to endure for eternity.

The Moral Law Is Useful

Finally, the biblical worldview maintains that God's moral law is useful. The point here is that God's moral law is not ethereal and abstract, but temporal and concrete. In other words, God's law is relevant to our lives in this world. It is not just some internal spiritual ideal to be contemplated by monks, but it is meant to be lived and embraced in this world.

Historically, Reformed theologians have spoken of three uses for God's moral law. The first is its ability to reveal our sin and subsequent need of a Savior. The moral law is useful in diagnosing the ailment of our souls and pointing us to the cure. The second use of the moral law is its ability to restrain sin in our civil society by providing culture with stark boundaries regulating human behavior. The third and final use of the moral law is as a guide for holy living. The moral law of God is like a divine GPS device that allows us to live wisely and please God. Those who love God will long to pursue righteousness in gratitude for their redemption.

The biblical worldview is that there is one unchanging, universal, and useful standard for morality—God's moral law, which is summarized in the Ten Commandments. This moral standard is something knowable and certain. It reflects the very holiness of God, and it is authoritative in regulating human behavior in all ages and among all cultures.

The Worldview of the Adversary: It's All Relative

As we have seen, the biblical worldview calls us to recognize God's law as an immutable and timeless moral absolute setting apart right from wrong. As we would expect, the worldview of our adversary is diametrically opposed to God's law and instead calls us to establish a new law founded on our personal discretion and autonomy. The worldview of our adversary advocates moral relativism, in which right and wrong are solely determined by the whims of our personal preference. This worldview is having a devastating impact on both our culture and the church.

Relativism and Our Culture

It would be a gross understatement to say that the period of the judges did not represent the glory days of Israel's history. That period of Israel's history revealed a cyclical pattern of unfaithfulness. One of Israel's problems during the period of the judges was that the people were engaged in a form of moral relativism. For example, in Judges 17:6 we read, "In those days Israel had no king; *everyone did as he saw fit*." The King James Version renders this verse as follows: "In those days there was no king in Israel, *but every man did that which was right in his own eyes*." During this period of Israel's history, people were not guided by God's unchanging moral standards; rather, they followed their own autonomously created moral guidance systems.

Our culture is engaging in the very same type of conduct. Everyone is doing as he or she sees fit; every person is doing what is right in his or her own eyes. The impact of this worldview on our culture is very similar to that experienced in Israel; we are suffering moral decay and paying the price for our unrighteousness. As the following quote suggests, this increasing level of moral decay is directly related to our cultural infatuation with relativism: "The death of truth in our society has created a moral decay in which every debate ends with the barroom question 'says who?'" When we abandon the idea that one set of laws applies to every human being, all that remains is subjective, personal opinion."[3] We see the concrete results of a "says who?" culture all around us. We see it in our culture's attempts to redefine human existence, its undermining of marriage, and its unbridled toleration of wickedness.

Relativism and the Church

Relativism has made significant inroads in the mind-set of the modern evangelical church. One of the great errors that the church has been prone to embracing is syncretism with the surrounding culture. It was true in the early church as many attempted to merge Christianity with Gnosticism. It is true in the modern church as many are attempting to merge Christianity with the principles of postmodernism, one of which is the denial that we can know absolute truth. This embracing of a form of relativism has found a strong foothold in the emerging church, which sees postmodernism as an opportunity to decouple Christianity from its perceived overreliance on propositional truth.[4] David Wells notes that emergents often parrot the mantras of relativists, saying things such as "We do not know," "We cannot know for sure," "No one can know certainly," "We should not make judgments," and "Christianity is about the search, not about the discovery."[5]

The end result of this trendy embracing of relativism is a watering down of the very foundation of Christianity. Christianity is constructed on the unflinching reality that absolute

---

3. Quotation recorded in *The Presbyterian Layman*, July–August 1996, 8.

4. D. A. Carson describes this trend in his book *Becoming Conversant with the Emerging Church*. See particularly pages 31–36.

5. David Wells, *The Courage to Be Protestant* (Grand Rapids: Eerdmans, 2008), 77.

truth is knowable through the self-revelation of God. In a misguided effort to be relevant, the emerging church is actually undermining the gospel through an unwise self-inflicted wound. David Wells issues the following stern warning to those who think biblical Christianity can accommodate relativism: "Those in the evangelical church today who are being lured by the siren call of postmodern relativism, who are increasingly uncertain that truth can be known, or that it matters all that much anyway, would do well to ponder the fact that this uncertainty goes to the very heart of what Christianity is all about."[6] The church that embraces relativism is a church that rejects biblical Christianity, and the ramifications are being widely felt in the Christian world. Doctrine is being neglected. Piety is declining. The lines that define the boundaries of orthodoxy are being blurred. The gospel is being watered down and recast. Relativism in the church is eroding the authority of biblical truth.

Combatting Relativism: Tearing Down the Stronghold of Relativism's Two Lies

If Christians are to resist the pernicious onslaught of relativism in the culture and the church, we must expose the two major foundational lies on which the house of relativism is built—that objective and absolute truth is unknowable and that "true truth" is avoidable.

Lie #1: Truth Is Unknowable

The first lie of the relativist is that objective and absolute truth is unknowable. According to the relativist, no human being can possess an objective understanding of truth, and thus no one is able to make absolute judgments of right and wrong. The relativist maintains that all humans are hobbled by the fact that they are always in possession of partial aspects of

6. Ibid.

the truth. Each culture and each individual has only a portion of truth, and thus no culture and no individual can claim to speak authoritatively for all.

One of the favorite illustrations used by relativists to make the point that objective and absolute truth is unknowable is the story of the blind men and the elephant.[7] In this story, six blind men approach an elephant, and each of them encounters a different part of his body. The first blind man comes up against the elephant's flat and sturdy side and concludes that an elephant is essentially a wall. The second blind man grabs the sharp end of the elephant's tusk and decides that an elephant is like a spear. The third man grasps the elephant's trunk and opines that an elephant is like a snake. The fourth encounters the elephant's leg and resolves that an elephant is like a tree. The fifth touches the elephant's thin flapping ear and theorizes that an elephant is like a fan. The final blind man takes hold of the elephant's thin tail and determines that an elephant is like a rope.

The relativist argues that we are like the blind men in this story when it comes to knowing truth. Each individual and culture touches upon the truth, but mistakenly believes that it has all the truth. In reality, according to the relativist, we are really in possession of only part of the truth, and thus none of us can speak authoritatively on right and wrong. We are all ignorant of the big picture, and thus our pontifications on absolute truth are merely a form of emotive babbling. Consider how John Godfrey Saxe concludes his poetic version of the story of the blind men and the elephant:

And so these men of Indostan
Disputed loud and long,
Each in his own opinion

7. This story appears in many different versions, languages, and cultures. I am drawing this version of the story from John Godfrey Saxe's poem "The Blind Man and the Elephant."

Exceeding stiff and strong,
Though each was partly in the right,
And all were in the wrong!

So oft in theologic wars,
The disputants, I ween,
Rail on in utter ignorance
Of what each other mean,
And prate about an Elephant
Not one of them has seen!

According to the lie of the relativist, no one has seen the entire elephant of truth, and thus no one knows what is objectively right or wrong.

On one level, I agree with the conclusion of the relativists that absolute truth is entirely unknowable by unaided human reason. Man in his natural state has a darkened mind that has been impaired by the noetic effects of sin. Like the men groping the elephant, we are all born blind.

But the error made by the relativists is their failure to factor God into the equation. God is *not* blind and he *is* all-knowing. He is a perfect moral being with unimpaired judgments. It is impossible for him to convey anything but perfect truth to us. David Wells comments on the difference between humanity and God when it comes to knowing the truth: "We are sometimes deceitful and untruthful, but this is quite impossible with God. He cannot be other than what he is as holy. He cannot have given us 'truth' that is untrue. And because he is all-knowing, and has known the end from the beginning, it is impossible for him to be mistaken as humans often are."[8] While humans can't know all the truth, God does, and he has revealed it to us through his Word. In other words, the blind men would know what an elephant was if the elephant chose to reveal this truth to them. In this circumstance, even blind

8. Wells, *The Courage to Be Protestant*, 75.

men could understand the truth. What is required in order to know the truth is divine self-revelation. This is what Christians possess in the Bible.

If Christians are to tear down the strongholds of relativism, we must point to the elephant that speaks. We must point people to the God of truth and escort people into the power of his Word. We must admit to people that when it comes to truth, we do see through a glass darkly, but at the same time we must inform them of the One who has revealed all truth to us. This is exactly what the apostles did as they encountered the paganism of the world around them. They witnessed to the truth. Like the apostles, we must counter the lie that truth is unknowable with the truth of the God who is knowable and who has revealed to us all we need for faith and life. We must testify to the absolute truth of the gospel of Jesus Christ.

Lie #2: "True Truth" Is Avoidable

The second great lie of the relativist is that "true truth" is avoidable. "True truth" is the term Francis Schaeffer gave to the objective, absolute, and God-revealed truth that Christians possess in the Bible. My point here is that relativists long to believe that absolute moral truth is something they can escape. Subconsciously, relativists know that there really is "true truth" out there, but they suppress this truth because they want to live like Israel in the days of the judges: they want to do whatever is right in their own eyes.

Relativism offers our culture the illusory elixir of personal autonomy. Relativism offers us the attractive lie that we can live according to our own moral compass and that there will be no repercussions. Like Adam, we all prefer to make our own laws, as opposed to submitting to God's law. We are by nature creatures inclined to self-rule. Ultimately, we are inclined to embrace moral relativism because it allows us to satisfy our personal sinful desires. Moral relativism ostensibly offers the ability to reclassify evil things as morally indifferent. It also allows us to marginalize God and reduce our personal sense of guilt. As Francis Beckwith and Gregory Koukl note, this makes moral relativism extremely attractive because "relativists seem to think [that] if they can get rid of both morality and God, then guilt and judgment will disappear as well."[9]

But the problem with moral relativism is that it is a facade. It doesn't change anything. We can't simply close our eyes and think God's law, sin, guilt, and judgment will disappear. According to Beckwith and Koukl, attempting to get rid of morality and God in order to get rid of our guilt and judgment is "like saying [that] if we can eliminate doctors and hospitals, then disease and suffering will disappear too."[10] Such thinking is not only foolish, but ultimately self-destructive. Moral relativism is like giving a dying man a placebo; it guarantees only death.

The only remedy for the underlying problem that moral relativism attempts to mask is Jesus Christ. The only way for us to be in accord with God's moral law and to deal with our sin, guilt, and judgment is to embrace, through the gift of faith, the person and work of Christ. By means of the imputation of Jesus' righteousness, we are counted as perfectly righteous; and by means of his sacrificial death, we are no longer numbered among the condemned. This is why it is imperative for the church to avoid watering down the glory of God's law and the ugliness of our sin. The church must speak boldly about these realities to a culture immersed in sissified forms of tolerance that avoid speaking truth. It is the church's calling to prophesy to this age by unmasking this lie of moral relativism and offering the balm of the gospel in its stead.

As Christians, we must actively resist the lies of relativism. We must take this thought captive to Christ. We must hold fast to "true truth" in an age that longs to serve the interests of the Father of Lies.

9. Francis J. Beckwith and Gregory Koukl, *Relativism: Feet Firmly Planted in Mid-Air* (Grand Rapids: Baker, 1998), 170.
10. Ibid.

Not All Values Are Created Equal

In the introduction to this chapter, I referred to HSBC's advertising campaign that attempted to advocate for moral relativism. The goal of the campaign was to suggest that all moral perspectives are equally worthy of consideration. The interesting thing is that HSBC found it very difficult to avoid favoring certain values over others. HSBC could not help but insert its own judgments on topics such as labor unions, immigration, and environmental policy. Eric Felten, writing in a *Wall Street Journal* editorial, noted that while HSBC tried to practice moral relativism, it ultimately made a judgment that favored some values over others: "But the judgment creeps in nonetheless: All values may be equal, in HSBC's view, but some are more equal than others."[11]

This is the problem with moral relativism: it's impossible to practice. Not all values are equal, and this means that some power, be it the government or a multinational corporation, must make a moral judgment. The question for us is this: Whom do we want to make moral judgments for us? Do we want to place this decision in the hands of an all-knowing and benevolent God who never errs in his judgments or in the hands of humanity, whose faculties, minds, and hearts are clouded by the impact of sin?

Beckwith and Koukl are right to suggest that in the end we all must accept one of the two following alternatives: "Either relativism is true or morality is true. Either we live in a universe in which morality is a meaningless concept and thus we are forever condemned to silence regarding any moral issue, or moral rules exist and we're beholden to a moral God who holds us accountable to his law. There are no other choices."[12] The choice for those maintaining a biblical worldview is clear.

11. Eric Felten, "A Bank Raises Interest—But Loses Values," *Wall Street Journal On-Line Edition*, August 16, 2009.

12. Beckwith and Koukl, *Relativism*, 170.

Anthony Selvaggio is an ordained minister, a lawyer, an author, a lecturer, and a visiting professor at Ottawa Theological Hall, Ottawa, Canada. He received his Juris Doctor (J.D.) from the University at Buffalo School of Law and his Masters of Divinity from the Reformed Presbyterian Theological Seminary. Previously he was a visiting professor at the Reformed Presbyterian Theological Seminary in Pittsburgh. He edited and contributed to *The Faith Once Delivered: Essays in Honor of Dr. Wayne R. Spear*. He lives in Rochester, New York, with his wife, Michelle, and his two children, Katherine and James.